[illegible] view of Plymouth Church Sunday School, Brooklyn, N. Y.

Our Sunday School:

AND

HOW WE CONDUCT IT.

BY

WALDO ABBOT.

WITH

AN INTRODUCTION,

BY JOHN S. C. ABBOTT.

BOSTON:
HENRY HOYT,
NO. 9 CORNHILL.

1863

INTRODUCTION.

By Rev. John S. C. Abbott.

THE Sabbath School has proved itself to be emphatically the nursery of the church. Wherever there is a well conducted Sabbath School with its system of Bible classes, there one invariably finds the organized church in a flourishing condition. There seems to be here developed almost as regular a progression of cause and effect, as in any of the works of nature. God shows himself as ready to co-operate, with his divine blessing, in this sowing of the seed and gathering in of the harvest of spiritual husbandry, as in any of the more material labors in which men may engage.

The skillful superintendence of a Sabbath

School is an art of difficult attainment. It is a *gift* rather than an art. As Horace said of the poet, the superintendent is *born* such, not made. Some men have the innate capacity to superintend affairs. With comprehensive grasp they can embrace the totality of the School, with all its diversified interests, while, at the same time, not the minutest details of duty can escape their eagle glance. With tact, which God has given, they move, amidst their multifarious duties, unembarrassed, instinctively deciding, in every emergency, just what is to be done. As Cæsar chose his generals, always getting the right man for the right place, so they, by the unerring light of an inward consciousness, decide who shall take the infant class, who a class of refined and cultivated young ladies, and who shall tame a set of coarse, vulgar, unruly boys, and who shall guide the mature and thoughtful minds of Christian adults in the highest branches of theology. They know how to classify the pupils, so that congenial and harmonious characters shall be together.

Not a ragged boy can peep in at the door of such a school but he finds himself lured to the very class to which he naturally belongs, and to the care of a teacher who will not allow him to slip from his grasp. If there is a teacher absent, the eye of such a superintendent instantly discerns the fact, and the defect is promptly rectified. Or rather, a skillful superintendent inspires his corps of teachers with such zeal, that almost never is a teacher absent from his post without providing a suitable supply.

As the efficiency of an army depends mainly upon its general, so does the efficiency of a Sabbath School depend almost entirely upon its superintendent. The first thing to be done in organizing a Sabbath School is to get a good Superintendent. When Marshal Ney, in the retreat from Moscow, performed a wonderful feat of heroism, in which he rescued a division of the army from apparently inevitable destruction, Napoleon grasped him by the hand, exclaiming, "An army of deer, led by a lion, is better than an army of lions led by a deer."

As an able general will inspire all his subordinate officers and soldiers with heroism, throwing, as it were his own enthusiastic spirit into their bosoms, so an efficient superintendent, by the energies of his own mind, can inspire a whole school with that ardor which glows and burns in his own heart. Fortunately the free institutions of our land, our noble system of common schools, and the elevating influence of labor, as combined in our manufactories, has developed, in every village of our country, men equal to these responsibilities. Any man who would make a good general, a good colonel of a regiment, a good superintendent of a factory, a good merchant having twenty clerks in his employ, possesses the intellectual qualifications requisite for a good superintendent. He needs only piety and zeal to fit him fully for the office.

William Cowper, the poet, as superintendent of the Lee Avenue Sabbath School, in Brooklyn, with its two thousand pupils, would run that magnificent institution into remediless ruin in less than six weeks. But you might search Christendom in vain for a more admirable teacher than he for a Bible Class of refined and highly cultivated young ladies. The reformed and regenerated pugilist, fresh from the ale house and the prize ring, who has just learned to sing the songs of Zion, placed over such a class of young ladies, would drive them out of the church by the second Sabbath. But it is doubtful if one could find a more desirable teacher, for an untamed class of vagabond boys, from any of the streets of our great cities.

Our Sabbath Schools are now attracting the attention and enlisting the energies of our ablest men. The future hope of the nation is greatly centering in these nurseries of piety. It is very important that the teachers, in these Sabbath schools, should be familiar with the plans adopted, and with the results of experiments in other schools. The writer of the following treatise has had facilities, such as few have enjoyed, to visit schools widely throughout our land, and particularly to study the organization and the routine of the most celebrated and successful Schools existing among us. The suggestions contained in this volume are so eminently practical, and have proved so successful in actual operation, and they cover so widely all the wants of the Sabbath School, that it may safely be asserted that the book will prove of great value wherever read. The thoughts which are here presented are not visionary theories. The book is founded on the Baconian philosophy, giving facts, and the results of actual experiments.

All that is here suggested may not perhaps wisely be introduced into any one school. Each superintendent has his own peculiar characteristics, his own modes of action, and he cannot pursue any administrative policy in a line antagonistic to his own nature. But he cannot fail to find, in these pages, so rich in the record of the results of the labors of others, much to animate him, and to suggest to him that variety of thoughts and plans essential to the success of the Sabbath School.

The writer of this little treatise has, for some time, been the superintendent of a Sabbath School in New Haven, composed mainly of children from the most neglected classes in the community. In this school the principles contained in these pages, have been carried into action, with a degree of success which is quite wonderful, and which effectually invests this book with the character of a safe and practical guide.

JOHN S. C. ABBOTT.

New Haven, Conn., June, 1863.

OUR SUNDAY SCHOOLS.

CHAPTER I.

ON ORGANIZING A SCHOOL.

AT a Sunday School meeting a short distance from New Haven, a clergyman lately addressed the children as follows:

"Look at nearly all the great and good men for the last two or three hundred years. They received their early religious culture in the Sunday School."

It is unfortunate that this excellent example cannot be supported by facts. But as not quite a hundred years have passed since the first conception of a modern Sunday School, the gentleman was unwittingly a false teacher.

At the first organization of the Christian church, it is supposed that a certain degree of instruction was afforded to children, as a work called "The Church and House Book," composed by the early Christians, contained directions for their culture. The children were called "catechumens," and were, after a three years course of religious instruction, baptized and received into the church, as a matter of course. These schools existed until the eighth century, when they appear to have been discontinued. In 1527, Martin Luther organized several schools in Germany, which were, however, more secular, although they were instituted that the children "might thereby be better able to read the Holy Scriptures." In the latter part of the sixteenth century, Cardinal Borromeo organized a Sunday School in the Cathedral at Milan, and about the same time (1674,) one was established at Roxbury, Mass.

In 1763, there was in Catterick, Yorkshire, a good and pious curate, named T. Lindsey, who was rather a fanatic, and thought that children of the poor might be taught something. He therefore met them in the church an hour before afternoon service, and instructed them in morals, while his wife had two classes which she taught reading and writing, as well as virtue. About the same time, a friend of theirs, a Miss Harrison, who had seen the school, started one in her own kitchen at Bedale. She proved so popular a teacher that the room could not accommodate the scholars, and she was obliged to have a succession of classes, lasting nearly the whole day, save during church hours. She instructed them in Watts's shorter catechism, and taught them hymns. Still these services were more like lectures to the young than our present school.

At the same time, Sunday Schools for the

secular study of reading, writing, arithmetic, drawing, &c., were established in Paris, Vienna and Rome, for those whose occupations prevented their attending week-day schools. In these places, however, the Sunday School proper, has never flourished.

The modern Sunday School is usually ascribed to Robert Raikes, of Gloucester, England, an editor of some note. In 1781, he was struck with the miserable appearance of the children in the streets. Released from work and day-school, they were the pest of the neighborhood. He engaged several women who kept schools near by, to receive such children as he should send, and instruct them in reading and the catechism, for which he paid them a shilling a day. It was pretty much as one of the teachers said, "It is but little they pays me, and it's but little I teaches them." He became interested in the children, and his genial manners made him a great favorite with them. The good fruits were seen, and other schools sprang up all over England, the teachers of which were paid for their services. An article on the subject by Mr. Raikes, in 1783, in his Journal, brought the matter before the world, and was the real commencement of the Sunday School movement. Among the most prominent followers of Mr. Raikes, was a Quaker by the name of Joseph Lancaster, who, when eighteen years of age, established a school, and had ninety scholars whom he instructed himself. He devoted his life to educational objects, and was the means of establishing the Lancasterian schools still existing in England. In 1812, he came to the United States, where he died in 1838. In 1785, William Fox, merchant, of London, organized the "Society for Promoting Sunday Schools in the British Dominions," and in 1786, it was estimated that there were 250,000 children of Great Britain in the Sunday Schools.

In the same year, Bishop Asbury, of Virginia, established a school on Mr. Raikes' plan, and in 1791, the first school of any kind, was established in Philadelphia. It is stated that in 1793, a poor African woman, named Katy Ferguson, knowing nothing of Robert Raikes, or Sunday Schools, started the first one in New York City.* The first exclusively religious school in Massachusetts, was opened by a young lady, afterwards Mrs. Ebenezer Everett, at Beverly, in 1805. This lady was for life an energetic and successful teacher, and died a few years since in Brunswick, Maine.

The first school in connection with any church, was Pittsburg, Penn., in 1809. In most of these schools the teachers were hired, by which means a portion of their benefits were lost. Also the schools were merely for the degraded and pauper children. The change

*Appleton's Enc. Art. Sunday Schools.

from salaried to voluntary teachers was effected in the United States, in 1809.

In 1816, the New York Sunday School Union was established, and in 1824, the Amercan Sunday School Union. In 1861, there were in Great Britain and Ireland, 3,600,000 pupils, and 340,000 teachers in the various schools. In the same year it is estimated that there were in the United States, 3,000,000 pupils. At the present day, there are doubtless nearly 4,000,000 children in our Sunday Schools, and 400,000 teachers.

In France the Sunday School has never prospered. Many have been established, but have failed or degenerated into the mere secular instruction of artisans and others, unable to attend school on other days.

Our own beloved country, thanks to the energy of John Wesley and his followers, to whom we are more indebted than to any others, is now becoming well supplied with the little Sunday School. That noble, self-denying band of pioneer Methodist ministers, are leaving the traces of their labors at every frontier hut and clearing. Religion and progress are walking hand in hand, and the Sunday School will soon be, as the common school now is, our pride, strength and boast.

The Rev. Dr. William Adams, of New York, in a recent sermon, made an allusion to the death of his father, Rev. John L. Adams, LL. D., who was for many years the principal of Phillips Academy, at Andover. When over seventy years of age, after he had finished what was regarded as his life-work, and having settled down amidst the enjoyments and quiet of domestic life, his strength was renewed by a new form of Christian activity. By his own personal exertions, he organized in the State of Illinois, more than five hundred Sabbath Schools, in connection with which numerous Christian Churches now exist.

All know how wonderfully the Schools have

spread, and one can hardly walk any of the streets of our cities, without hearing some dirty-faced, bare-footed child singing, "I want to be an angel." Still the matter is in its infancy, and requires the careful attention of able men. A few years since, the writing of children's books was deemed fit occupation for very young ladies and weak-minded men. Now, some of the ablest and most vigorous intellects are devoted to children. But lately a man who was good for nothing, was deemed amply competent for a schoolmaster. Now, the children demand the wisest and most learned. Our Sunday School teachers are a little behind the times, not in zeal, but in the knowledge how to proceed, and a realization of the amount of preparation necessary for success in their undertaking.

The writer has visited schools from Canada to Texas; from the humble beginning in an attic, cramped by want of means, to the gathering from the avenues, where the vast and much-to-be-desired power of money has lent her aid to form, as far as possible, a "royal road to heaven." From what I have thus gathered, I propose to offer some brief practical advice on organizing and sustaining a Sunday School.

Each school must be distinctive in its general mode of conduct, as the children differ in age, intelligence, character, wealth, etc. In establishing a school, it is necessary to determine first, what class of children are likely to attend, whether rich or poor, intelligent or ignorant. If it be the regular school connected with the church, the establishment is comparatively simple, as the whole power of the church can be drawn upon for teachers and moral support.

After providing your room, obtain your teachers. If possible, always have one more teacher present than you have classes for.

It always has a very bad effect to allow a class to wait for a teacher. They will not do nothing. Unless they can do something *good*, they will certainly learn a long lesson in mischief. One or two paper balls thrown by boys waiting for a teacher, will often breed an insurrection, that several Sundays' bombardment with the catechism will not quell. A teacher by a single day's absence may do incalculable injury to his class.

An old story is told of two Irishmen who went to fish a kettle from a river. Mike was to lower himself and hold on to the bridge with his hands, while Pat was to hang on to his legs with one hand, and hook up the kettle with a pole. Just as Pat had got his pole into the water, Mike called out:

"Hould on, a bit, Pat, till I spit on me hands!"

The result can be demonstrated to any who may not at once see it.

There is often a moral to a joke, and not a whit more wise than Mike is a teacher who unnecessarily leaves his scholars for a session. He has lost part of his hold on them. The children are left to coin mischief, worry neighboring classes, and to feel that their teacher is tired of them. Or, if a substitute is provided, they dislike him, and are not bashful about showing it; or if they fancy him, it is so much of the teacher's power over them lost.

A superintendent must determine to give the same energy, care, and labor in building up a Sunday School, that he would in establishing any new business. Two hours' work on Sunday will never accomplish it. He must think of all sorts of novel plans for entertaining the children and drawing them in. Religion to most children is a pill, which they will not take unless it is sugar-coated.

For a Mission School, a room should be

provided as pleasant and comfortable as possible. If I were to have a hundred dollars to fit up a room, or to purchase a library, I would expend every dollar in painting the walls a pleasant tint, in providing comfortable cushions, and procuring such things as would make the Sunday School pleasanter and more cheerful than their homes. Make it a little heaven for them. If possible, get some of the worse boys in the neighborhood to help you fit up. This will make them feel an ownership in the property, and prevent their destroying it. They will deem it "our school," and woe to the fellow who touches their property. There are no police-officers so vigilant as half-civilized boys, who have had one good point cultivated. They can tell by the looks of a jack-knife whether it is intended to rip open a cushion, or to carve a "Heenan" on the wall; and are not diffident about requesting its proprietor to give up the game or the knife.

In entertaining company, a luxuriant easy chair, by a glowing fire, in a cozy, pretty room, will do wonders. Though you may hardly open your lips, save to give welcome, your guest pronounces yours a most delightful place to visit. So a pleasant, comfortable school-room will accomplish marvels in drawing and keeping scholars; and what is more, the threat of expulsion will give great power in discipline.

Various methods are employed to draw in scholars. The best way is to make the exercises entertaining, and there will usually be no difficulty in filling the room. Pour out the molasses, and the flies will find it. In small places, or where there are strong influences to keep children away, such as in a Roman Catholic neighborhood, it is well to have recourse to extraneous inducements. The most common is, to have a gingerbread supper on some week-day evening — an attraction so powerful that the children will attend in spite of a bull from the Pope himself. The children are to have so good a time that they will come to the school on Sunday from gratitude, or a desire for more good things. But woe unto you, if the next Sunday School is not a pleasant one. The childrens' imaginations are strung up, and the reaction from a dull season will be so great that you will see them no more.

Some years ago, I was walking down one of the avenues in New-York, in quest of a new Sunday School. Hearing some singing, I went up stairs and into a room beautifully furnished as a chapel. In the pulpit was a gentleman I had frequently seen wielding the auctioneer's mallet, and who, to say the least, was an exceedingly eccentric person. The singing ceased, and he took a text, from which he proceeded to preach a sermon, compensating in quantity for its lack in quality. His audience consisted merely of three boys and myself. Occasionally he would pause to ejaculate,

"You big boy, stop that now," or "you little boy, with a blue jacket, move to the end of the bench, and quit playing while I'm preaching."

At the close of the service, I remained, and congratulated him on his beautiful room, expressing some surprise that it was not better filled. It was the prettiest little Sunday School room I have ever seen. The gentleman seemed quite disheartened at his ill success, and wanted sympathy. I gave him what I could, and he showed me about the premises.

"I furnished the room at my own expense," said he, "and have worked hard to build up a school, but it does not please the Lord to grant me success."

"Well, sir, would it not be better to have your exercises more adapted to children's minds; make them more entertaining, and—"

"Ah, sir, there you have fallen into the great error of the times. All mankind seem to be mad on 'entertaining' children. Preachers preach 'entertaining' sermons. It is the infidelity of the age sir; yes sir, the infidelity of the age. It is doing vast injury. You must preach and teach 'Christ and him crucified,' and that alone."

"True," said I, trying to recall sundry editorials I had read on the subject, "but we must present the subject in an interesting manner, or people will not listen."

"Sir, we must *not* interest people; why, they would come to Church and Sunday School merely to be interested. The Sabbath is too holy a day, to occupy in 'interesting' people. Now here, every month or two, we have a fine supper of good things for the children, with addresses, etc., and sometimes we have three hundred children present," and his face lighted up at the thought; "why, the room is crowded full. But then, it is true that they do *not* turn out very well on Sunday. I suspect it is the Central Park that keeps them away."

After some more such conversation, I left. A few months after, I was passing, and took a look in through a small crack in the door. He was preaching "Christ and him crucified" still, and his audience had increased to nearly a dozen. I went on my way rejoicing at his success.

Children that run the streets will go where they have the best time. If they do not enjoy themselves at Sunday School, they will go skating or robbing orchards. Of course, where parental authority is exercised they will attend, as they would go to a dentist's, and if their hearts are not engaged, it is doubtful which place would benefit them most.

I once heard of a gentleman who gave an exhibition of a magic lantern, intending to have Scripture scenes, and give little moral plums with each picture.

I am unwilling to use such an exhibition on Sunday, as a Sabbath School lesson, but as a week-day amusement, find it one of the most popular of entertainments. A school must be under very perfect control, however, to render it safe to darken the room. I have seen such confusion occasioned by it, as to counterbalance any good the exhibition might do.

I have thought a good way would be to have a room pleasantly furnished with some fine engravings, such as the exquisite series of the "Voyage of Life," or the "Cartoons of Raphael." Then begin by explaining the pictures to the children. Show but one or two new ones each time, giving a practical application of the moral. As the number of pupils increases, divide them into classes, and let the teacher explain the pictures. By easy transition from studying the picture of the "Transfiguration," the class can be led to read the account of it from the Testament, and before they know it, they are at the purgatory of children — school.

It is well to present to the children, particularly the smaller ones, some little gift, such as a picture or a verse card. It will occasion more talk on the subject, and lead others in to obtain some for themselves. It is surprising to notice how early the bump of acquisitiveness is developed.

By all means avoid bribing the children to attend, by promising any extra inducement; that is, by offering an individual any more than all the pupils can have. I have known of money being offered to attract children. The gentleman who tried it realized his folly, on being stopped in the street by a little fellow, who said:

"I say, Mr., if ye'll give me six cents, I'll go to your Sunday School for a month."

Even in having entertainments, allow only the regular members of the school to be present; and then announce that at a certain time in the future, you will have another festival, to which all who join the school immediately, will be invited. Otherwise you will have a large roll of pupils who will attend merely for the loaves and fishes. Thus make your gifts rewards for work done, rather than bribes. Never pay in advance. It makes the children think that they confer a favor on the teachers by joining the school.

It is only by carefully watching the children, and being ready with something new, as soon as they are tired of the old, that a Sabbath School can be successfully conducted. There is a peculiar fascination in holding the wheel of a vessel, and feeling that our will can compel the huge mass to visit Canton or Liverpool, to bow to the ice-bergs, or nod to the equator. It is the charm of influencing matter, of command, of seeing the result of our own power. But there is a sweeter pleasure in moulding the minds of unruly boys, of seeing the slow but certain change from animals to men, guiding them so delicately that they shall not feel the curb, and in feeling not only that they are *growing* better, but that they *are* better — and it is "our handiwork."

CHAPTER II.

THE MECHANICAL PART OF A SCHOOL.

ON entering a large manufactory, one of the noticeable features is the perfect order and regularity which prevails. Everything runs by system. Each operator is but a part of the great machine. The huge driving-wheel of the engine moves not more according to rule, than the hundreds of workmen who throng the building. The superintendent has apparently nothing to do. The machine is "perpetual motion," and has received its start. But let a cog in a wheel be broken, and the superintendent knows it. Quietly he sees that it is repaired—not merely *orders* it done, but *attends to it.* The ability of such an officer consists in so perfecting details that his own services, to a casual observer, appear almost unnecessary.

A Sunday School requires the same perfect mechanism as a factory. Without it no school can be very prosperous or efficient. Many superintendents have an indefinite idea that they should be bustling about continually, to remind all that there is such an officer. The more a school can be made to run smoothly of itself the better. The superintendent should, as it were, go quietly around, oiling the joints, touching the springs, and learning the characteristics of teachers and scholars; willing the while to be unnoticed. He who can do this is in no danger of oblivion. If possible, call every one by name. It will give a great power to be able thus to designate the children. It pleases the good ones, and causes the bad to imagine that you know all about them.

In selecting a superintendent, great care

should be exercised to obtain one of administrative ability, and who does not wear squeaky boots. It is not always wisest to select the most cultivated, or the one usually deemed the most devotional. Not that I would cast the slightest slur on the importance of both these qualities. But he who is quick, ready, self-confident, with a clear head, and the ability to arrange and classify, with some imagination for devising novelties, — is the man for the post. As between A, a foreman in a large printing-office, and B, a village physician, or a retired minister, I would select A; for the reason that his regular business has accustomed him to habits of command, in planning the proper division of labor, and in working through others. The physician's and minister's ordinary occupation has not been of such a character as to develop these traits. Neither is much of what is termed "book-learning" necessary. The superintendent should never take a class, and therefore his defects in this respect will not be noticed. Be sure and select a *successful* man: one who takes hold of an impossibility and creates a fact out of it. Never appoint one of these real good, pleasant, inefficient men, who can help every one but themselves. They are not the men to drive. They are capital teachers, but poor directors. A good superintendent is exceedingly difficult to find. He requires a rare combination of energy, good nature, and perseverance. To manage a large school is *work* —hard, steady work — requiring a *man* to do it, and one who does not talk too much.

I think it is seldom or never the duty of the pastor to take charge of the school. A faithful minister has enough to perform in the proper care of his church. What more he does is at the expense of these primary duties.

Invidious comparisons are sometimes drawn between the sermons of the clergy, and the literary productions of the lecturer, or the elaborate appeals of the advocate. It should be remembered, however, that the lawyer may occupy a month in preparing an eloquent and convincing address which renders him famous. The lyceum lecture is usually the fruit of half a year's thought, while the clergyman has to prepare two or three sermons a week. His mind has to exhale in driblets. He has no time for that mature elaborating and revising of his addresses which usually give them vitality. He must visit the sick, bury the dead, prepare for the prayer meeting, comfort the sorrowing, and above all, worry his life long, how to make both sides of his ledger balance. A man who can do these, and yet prepare two fresh, instructive, living sermons a week, cannot be deemed mediocre. He is doing well, a *great man's* work. I am not a clergyman, and therefore I can say that I know of no profession where the standard of ability is so high, or where, considering these impediments, there are so many examples of transcendent genius.

Do not, therefore, lay another burden upon your pastor's shoulders, or allow him to assume it. What interest he can manifest by his occasional presence, his influence, and his kindly word, he should, and he will always do. If you ask more, you are weakening his sermons — skimming the milk which you desire and need, for your own nutrition.

I speak earnestly, for I read many articles calling on ministers to lead the teachers' meetings, conduct Bible classes, and even to superintend the school. If you want him to perform merely the pastoral duties of a missionary, this may do. If you desire a preacher, with a mind to guide and instruct you; to enable you to be useful in the Sunday School, then allow him leisure to replenish a brain already far too often drawn upon.

Probably the best government, were all men honest, would be a large legislative power, and a one man administrative power. Certainly in a Sunday school this is indispensable.

I was once connected with a large school, where a noble man was spoiled into a poor superintendent. He was so kind-hearted that I believe he would have deemed it cruel to kick a football. He was so careful of the feelings of others, that it was difficult to learn what he desired the teachers to do. It was a five minutes' labor for him to persuade and coax the children into semi-silence. He would jingle his bell and talk to them imploringly, and finally, in a voice intended to be terrible, threaten to "attend to those boys who were kicking their feet on the benches." At this all laughed, until it became too stale even for a joke.

Boys like promptness and military precision.

Give a boy an order in a pleasant, but prompt, distinct, curt manner, and he is twice as likely to obey, as when it is given in a slipshod, half-beseeching air. A horse will at once tell who is afraid of him. Surely a boy has more intelligence. Often the form of a command will betray the conviction that it will be disobeyed.

Not long since I was in a mission-school where usually there was excellent order. The superintendent was away, and the assistant took his place. Chaos reigned supreme, and the bell was continually jingling. At the close of school, the acting superintendent said: "Now, boys, I want you to go out in your usual orderly manner. Your superintendent will be pleased to hear you have done so well to-day. Now go quietly, girls first." Habit restrained the boys for a moment, but when the girls got fairly into the aisles, they broke, and leaping over benches in perfect confusion, made for the door. A few got out, when a stranger, a small, light-built young man, stepped before the door, and gently laid his hands on two of the nearest boys. He merely called out "boys," loud enough to attract attention, and shook his head slightly. They knew what he meant, and instantly order was restored. The girls passed out, and the boys followed quietly. There is much in the strange magnetic influence, which some persons possess.

A horse that has once run away with you cannot be depended on. Never allow a school to break. You cannot regain your power. The children must be trained to obey quickly and perfectly. The lesson of obedience is one of the most important that children can be taught anywhere. It can be easily done — if you only know how. It is as simple as to set up Columbus' egg.

In calling the attention of the school, ring

the bell loud enough for all to hear, but on no account ring it more than once. If you do, the next time the children will anticipate a second bell, and continue their conversation accordingly. If a scholar persists in conversation or noise, call his name, or so designate him as to attract attention to him. Rarely will one require to be thus reproved twice.

The superintendent should seldom address the children, except on matters connected with the business of the school. They must know that when he speaks, it is to give orders which are to be *obeyed.* Moreover, his turn of mind becomes too familiar to the children, and they desire a change. Unless he can devote more attention to preparing his remarks than most men do, under the same circumstances, they will become stale, and encourage among the children habits of inattention to his voice, prejudicial to his influence.

I place most of the government on the superintendent, for the number of persons who are disciplinarians are extremely few. In most Sunday schools, not more than three or four have this ability. It is so rare in the world, that it is a wonder, not that so many children are ruined, but that so many blunder into the right path. A superintendent who expects each teacher to enforce order in his class, will have a noisy school. All teachers who *can* keep order should do so, but they are few. Many who can impart knowledge admirably, hardly know how to compel a boy to remove his cap.

Where the school is large, it is well to call the roll of the teachers. The assistant superintendent will call it, and the superintendent will answer for the lady teachers, who may dislike to reply in a sufficiently loud voice to be heard across the room. This custom will prove a great check upon tardiness and absence. If a teacher is away and has provided a substitute, it is well to say, "Miss Jones, absent; has provided a substitute." If a teacher is detained by illness, it is wise to state it.

The superintendent should, if possible, let others lead in prayer, that his attention may still be directed to keeping perfect order. It is seldom or never that a school is so well drilled that some will not be in mischief when the superintendent's and teachers' eyes are closed. He should let all know that his eyes are open and upon them.

At prayer all the teachers and scholars should take some uniform position, either inclining forward, or rising and folding the hands. For small children the latter is preferable, as it keeps their hands out of mischief. In any case the teachers should take the same position as the scholars, to show that the posture is not inconsistent with the dignity of a gentleman or lady. The teachers should be prompt to observe all such general forms. It is, I believe, a maxim even of our theology, that men are more easily taught by example than by precept. The teachers can induce their pupils to do almost anything, if they will only do it first.

In the class, the teacher should be left as nearly supreme as the general interests of the school will allow. If he much prefer, let him select his own lessons, and manage in his own way. The superintendent should carefully refrain from worrying a teacher, and from giving any orders to the class save through him. For instance, if he wants two boys to take part in the Sunday School Concert, instead of speaking to them personally, request the teacher to do so. It weakens a teacher's influence to have any one appear to be above him in authority over his own class. The teacher, also, should be very careful always to support the authority of the superintendent. If the boys are inclined to laugh at any little weakness he may have, stop it at once, and, if possible, present his foibles in a light to make them virtues. These are little matters, but they constitute the smooth finish of a school's mechanism.

After the opening exercises, the first duty of the superintendent will be, to supply unprovided classes with teachers. Usually he has to take any one who happens to be present. Where there is any choice, give the best teacher to the worse class. Where no teacher can be obtained, if the children of the class are reliable, let them hear each other's lessons, and then read part of a certain chapter in the Bible. Frequently a class of girls can be so managed for some time, pleasantly to themselves, and cause no trouble to any one. If the class be of boys, rather boiling over with fun and spirits, separate them. If you think of nothing better, tell them you want their help. Send two to the librarian, who will manage to keep them employed. Tell the others you want to know how many are present. Give each a pencil and paper, and let them walk very quietly down the aisles — each taking one — counting the teachers and scholars. Have them write the result neatly on paper, in as formal a manner as possible. This will effectually separate the class, and be a great delight to the boys, who always like to "help' when it is a little public in manner. If they finish too soon, tell them you wish it very accurate, and they had better go over it again to verify it. They will give great assurance of its correctness, but the next count will produce such a different result, that they will have sufficient employment for the hour. Receive the report with many thanks, and ostentatiously put it in a very secure place. Boys are in the main good, only they must have something to do. They prefer to be useful, but if they cannot have a chance, they will take up mischief.

Some care should be exercised in arrangeing the classes. Usually the only system is in having the girls on one side of the room, and the boys on the other. A capital method of making trouble. I never could understand why it is so proper for ladies and gentlemen to mingle at home, in company, at public meetings, and at church, yet so often in the prayer-meeting and Sunday School they are separated, like the sheep and the goats, before their time. Being among the goats, it has always suggested unpleasant emotions.

The classes should be so arranged as to bring those most troublesome, near the superintendent, where he can easily see them. Place the Bible Classes, and those with efficient teachers, farthest away. Do not have two classes of boys about the same age within speaking distance. Neither would I advise having a class of *young*, young ladies, side by side, with one of juvenile young men, lest they might agree with Mr. Pope, that "the proper study of mankind is man," and pursue that study to the detriment of others.

Unless necessary, do not have more than six pupils to one teacher. It is as many as most can manage and instruct. In the Bible classes there can be as many as can easily hear the teacher's voice.

Every class should be numbered, for ease in reference. In many schools the children are numbered also, for purposes hereafter explained.

Each teacher should keep a class-book, well and punctually written up. It is a somewhat difficult matter to have attended to, and therefore most superintendents let it go. Never let *anything* be done in a slip-shod manner. Either abolish the rule, or enforce it. When the books are well kept, they are of great assistance, and will repay the slight trouble of looking after them.

The most important duty of the superintendent is, in smoothing the path for the teachers, and encouraging them when disheartened. All teachers will at times become discouraged, and feel inclined to abandon their labors. It is truly hard to work month after month, with no apparent fruits; to feel that they are accomplishing nothing, and perhaps are only doing an injury. A superintendent should carefully watch for these symptoms, and be ready with a kind and inspiriting word; notice their classes frequently, with a word of commendation; refer to any good points they exhibit, either in order or recitation; keep their spirits up, and show himself willing to be a personal friend, yet with great care to avoid intruding himself. Here all the delicacy and Christian refinement he possesses should be brought into action, influenced by the divinest attribute given to man — LOVE.

CHAPTER III.

THE FORMAL EXERCISES OF A SCHOOL.

IT is a great blessing to the Sunday School that the old strong feeling of denominationalism has so greatly diminished — a feeling which but lately caused one sect to believe that a custom introduced by another, from that very fact, must be the device of the devil. The better the custom, the more sure were its opponents that none but Satan could contrive such a cunning invention to tempt the unwary from the true church. Unfortunately, however, we are not all saints yet, and a little of this "original sin" remains hidden, to come out on especial occasions. Some one has said:

"It is well that we are not all perfect; if

we were, we should be so intolerably proud of it, that there would be no getting along with us."

A short time since, I was on a Committee for decorating our church at Christmas. As it was a Congregational Society, it occasioned a little talk, as to its orthodoxy. It would have been perfectly correct to have sent artists to paint the wreaths and festoons in fresco; but being too poor for that, we were obliged to supply the handiwork of God, prepared by willing hands, to ornament the house of their Maker.

We designed to have a moss-covered cross back of the pulpit, with a stuffed dove descending on it. Around the walls were to be evergreen stars, etc. Of course, the congregation dropped in during the week, to see how the work progressed. One good man, a retired minister, earnestly remonstrated against having the cross. "It will not do, sir. It is imitating Popery." Another brother button-holed me, to protest against having the dove. It was an insult to the Holy Spirit. A third liked the design all but the stars, which were "out of place just now, reminding one of the 'Star Spangled Banner,' and all that sort of thing." To the credit of both the church and the gentlemen, a little pleasant conversation caused them to waive their objections, and acquiesce in the arrangements.

The plans suggested in this chapter will doubtless be exceedingly disapproved of by many. They are the best I have yet thought of, and objectors can easily disregard them. I ask, however, that we take any form, ceremomy, sermon, hymn, or tune, which is likely to assist in the saving of souls, from any sect or source, and appropriate it to our use, without any regard to its origin. An infidel, Voltaire, originated the first Tract Society. Surely, we should not object to draw forms and ceremonies from Christian denominations merely because we prefer our own creed.

> " Seek truth where'er it may be found,
> Among thy friends, among thy foes;
> On Christian or on heathen ground,
> The flower 's divine, where'er it blows."

In the formal exercises of a school, children can only be kept interested by taking an active part themselves. It is not children only who prefer talking to listening to the discourse of others. I think a very short service, adapted to children's minds, and somewhat after the Episcopal form, if really ably prepared, would be a desideratum. Let there be a plenty of movement and singing. I know many think that such a course would tend to make mere formalists of them. I see no reason for such a supposition; but if the exercise will interest the children more, bring them into the Sunday School, and tend to their conversion, is it not better to run some risk of this in making the more Christians? We must have some form, and why not a pleasant one, interesting and instructive to the children?

A Quaker met an acquaintance in whose church had recently been placed a superior organ. The Quaker congratulated him on its fine quality. His acquaintance expressed surprise that he could congratulate him for an act that he deemed wrong.

"Why, friend, if thou dost worship thy God by machinery, it is well that thou dost have a fine instrument."

If we are to have any machinery, any forms, any ceremony, in our schools, let us have them all of first class. Children require different things to interest and affect them from men, just as they require different clothes. A very short but diversified formula, with living, breathing prayers, is the best. For myself, I prefer the simple, dignified, unpretending service of the "meeting-house." For children, I prefer a certain degree of pomp and ceremony.

Pending the production of such a service, a programme as follows, is good:

1st. Call the roll of teachers.

2d. Sing. Singing should be frequent, and only one or two verses — seldom more than two at a time. The children should always rise and stand in singing.

3d. Let the superintendent read a portion from the Scriptures, the children reading the alternate verses, led by the assistant, who should stand at the further end of the room. Though this may injure the effect of some of the passages, yet it will keep the attention of the school, which is more important. Care should be taken in selecting the passages to have them adapted to their comprehension — such as the history of the creation, the lives of Daniel, Noah, Joseph, the parables of Christ, etc. The same subject can be continued from Sabbath to

Sabbath, when too long for one reading. A story that inculcates virtue is more likely to produce an impression than a mere command to be virtuous. From fifteen to twenty verses should be read at a time, which will occupy about two minutes.

4th. Sing.

5th. A prayer of not more than three minutes, concluding with the Lord's Prayer, repeated by the school in concert. When a stranger leads in prayer, if he omit the Lord's Prayer at his conclusion, the assistant should instantly commence it. The children anticipating it, there will be no confusion after the first time. They should have some uniform position. If old enough, let them incline their heads forward. If not, let them stand.

6th. Sing.

7. Repeat the ten commandments in concert, all standing. If the exercises are carried off promptly, this introductory service will occupy about twenty minutes.

8th. The study of the lessons. About three minutes before time to close, strike the bell as a warning, that the teachers may have time to conclude their remarks. At the moment for closing, strike the bell again, and conversation must instantly cease. A teacher should stop even in the middle of a sentence.

9th. Sing two verses.

10th. Close with one or two choice texts, repeated in concert, all standing. It is well to have the same daily, that they may be learned and recited by all, whether they can read or not. Such passages as the following are good:

"Let the words of my mouth, and the meditation of my heart, be acceptable in thy sight, O Lord, my strength and my Redeemer."—Psalm xix.

"The Lord watch between me and thee when we are absent one from another."—Gen. xxxi. 49.

There should be a moment's perfect silence, and then the school, at the tap of the bell, can be dismissed.

Unless many of the children are unable to read, do not read more than the first two lines of the hymn. In fact, at any time, it is a useless custom which it would be wise to abolish in the Sunday School, as only familiar hymns are sung. It is comparatively seldom that a hymn is so read as to be of any pleasure or profit. These exercises can be varied so as to occupy what time may be desired.

There should be a door-keeper, to prevent children running in during the exercises, interrupting the prayers and music. It is sin gular that no serviee can be made so interesting that people will not turn around to see who comes in late.

One Sunday in February, I was sitting on the piazza of an hotel in Texas, and amused myself telling stories to the children I had gathered around me. I told them that where I came from, there were one or two feet of snow on the ground, and that the rivers were all frozen so that men and horses could walk over on the ice.

"Well, I reckon ye can't come none of ye'r yankee stories over us," exclaimed the oldest, a boy of fourteen, with his hands perpetually in his pockets. All my efforts could not overcome their incredulity. They had not seen the wonder, and would not believe it.

But after all, most of us are as sceptical. Few will believe what personal experience has not proven. I ask you, however, to make a trial of this plan before you entirely condemn its working.

CHAPTER IV.

ON LESSONS AND CLASSES.

TEACHERS are often perplexed about the best mode of instructing and interesting their classes; what question book, if any, should be used; and how to occupy the time after hearing the lesson.

The burden of this book is, "Make the Sunday School interesting." So the lessons must be made interesting, or the children will derive but little benefit.

A story is told of a boy who said that on Sunday his grandmother used to tie him to the bed-post, to keep him out of mischief while she was at church, and set him learning the hymn, "Thine earthly Sabbaths, Lord,

I love." This mode of stimulating love cannot be commended as popular.

The mode of entertaining a class must, of course, differ according to circumstances. One class is of sober, thoughtful, intelligent children, who can be interested in the solemn truths of the Bible. They can appreciate, to a certain extent, the love of Christ, the beauty of his life, the grandeur of the plan of salvation. These facts move them. Their hearts are warm with love to men and to God — only they do not know it. They merely want the love of Christ brought before them; his mercy and sufferings. These feed their souls and supply the cravings of their hearts. They want no amusing stories told them — a tear over Calvary is sweeter than all the jokes of Hood. There are some few who seem born with so little "original sin," that it is invisible to the naked eye.

But here is a class of rough, brutalized

boys, picked up from the dens of New York, dirty and foul of soul as of shirt. What can they understand about the "beauty of holiness," the teachings of Christ's life. Their education is such that they would despise him for surrendering himself without showing fight. They cannot appreciate the grandeur of the sacrifice. How will they be benefitted or interested in learning "What is the chief end of man?" Theirs is a life of action; they cannot think. The art of thinking has to be learned as much as the art of talking. They find it impossible to follow a finished essay on "justification by faith," and hardly can the Christian virtues be made comprehensible to them.

Of course these two classes must be treated differently, yet we find one person advocating having a good, jolly time in Sunday Schools, and another arguing that not a smile should be allowed in the room.

Each teacher must *study* his class. If the scholars are low in the moral scale, he must appeal to and instruct their lower natures. A missionary on going to a heathen land, would probably preach in favor of wearing pantaloons before he explained the distinction between Calvinism and Arminianism, or even the advantages of Old or New-Schoolism. So a teacher should at first work away at the grosser sins, to try to stimulate the healthy action of the moral system.

The old mode of resuscitating, — or rather of killing — a half-drowned man, was by the counter-irritant method of hanging him up by the heels to let the water run out of him. Now, however, to the joy of all patients, the treatment is to lay the body flat and rub the extremities briskly, warming them well with hot bricks and blankets. What is this for? To stimulate the circulation.

Now these rough boys are "dead in sin."

We cannot pour it out of them. We must stimulate the moral circulation, and get them in a healthy state. Begin by rubbing the extremities, viz., preach temperance, virtue, and truth, appealing not only to the Bible to prove the necessity of these qualities,—for they virtually do not believe the Bible,—but to facts which they know, and to the teacher's own experience, which at first they will believe before the Bible. This is but teaching morality, it is true, but morality is better than vice.

Some say, "Why stop to lop off the branches one by one. Cut down the whole tree of sin at once. Teach them to 'love the Lord their God,' and it is done."

True, but often there is a dense underbrush to be cleared away before you can swing your ax at the trunk. In breaking a colt, it would be shorter to break him at once in a carriage, so as to have the whole thing quickly finished. The only trouble is, that it can't be done. You have first to break to halter, then to harness, then under the saddle, and, last of all, to the carriage. So with boys: break off their evil habits, and then there is a chance of making them Christians.

"An absence of sin is no more religion than an absence of weeds is harvest."

The teacher must work his way into the hearts of these boys, and a long, hard, sickening work it is. He must teach them who God is, and what he requires, before asking them to accept him. He meets the masked batteries of ignorance, selfishness, and pride, all well manned, at every step. It will not do to meet them with "glittering generalities," telling them to be good, and to do good. The boys wont stand it. He must address them with force, bring up facts to prove, and interesting stories to illustrate. His diamonds need not be polished, but they must be genuine. Keep their attention fixed by good religious instruction, if possible: but if not, tell them anything which will accustom their minds to concentration on any one subject.

I once told my class the story of Aladin's Lamp as a Sunday School lesson, imitating the original narrator and the popular story-paper in breaking off at exciting points and promising to continue. I mentioned the fact at the teachers' meeting, and noticed some sober faces, expressive of dislike of radical fanatics; but the result has confirmed my opinion that *in this case* it was the best course *I knew how* to pursue. It cemented the class, which was on the point of disbanding, and got them in the habit of regular attendance. At first it was merely to hear the story, but soon I was enabled to advance a step higher, and get them interested in Bible stories. Such boys must be interested. It is better to gather them together to read *Punch*, than to let them hang around grog-shops.

I do not advise bringing fun into the Sunday School. Every teacher must take that course which he believes right and best.

"'Tis with our judgment as our watches, none go just alike, yet each believes his own."

If possible, the exercises should be solemn and impressive: yet there are probably only about a dozen people in the country who can so conduct them, and interest the whole school. Most people have not this power, and must resort to poorer methods to accomplish their ends. I therefore say, interest your class and keep their attention by a direct teaching of the Gospel of Christ if you can: but with no fear of doing wrong if you have to cause a religious smile, or even a genuine honest laugh. It is something to teach a boy to laugh honestly.

The teacher should prepare his lesson carefully. He who is unwilling to take this trouble in his Master's service is unfit for the post.

He should plan his lesson, arrange his illustrations, and think over attentively what he will say. Let him select some one in his class, and arrange his lesson so that it shall be a personal appeal to him to repent of his sins. He should resolve to try to convert them that day — not next month or year, but *that day*, and strive with the energy that a belief of success inspires. He may not have success, but it may be that he will have planted the seed which will grow long after he has forgotten it. We never see the sprouting of a seed. He should throw himself into the spirit of the lesson, and let his whole soul strive for the end. It is hardly necessary to add, that no lesson is properly prepared without a fervent prayer for a divine blessing upon it. Yet how seldom it receives this indispensable attention. Haydn wrote, "When I was occupied on the 'Creation,' always before I sat down to the piano, I prayed to God with earnestness that he would enable me to praise him worthily."

I believe that the reason why female teachers are, as a general rule, the most successful, and that girls are more frequently converted than boys, is to be attributed to the fact that they are more devotional than men. A lady teacher seldom forgets to ask a blessing on her labors, and she receives corresponding fruit.

It is no small task to prepare a lesson properly, to plan everything so that it will pass off smoothly. It will not do to have poor, stupid religious truisms. "Pious trash is demoralizing."

A few weeks since, I heard a very superior teacher talking to her class. She was suddenly seized with a desire to make some remarks on commencing the new year; but not having bestowed upon the subject her customary attention, the boys were restless, and thinking of other matters. She was reminded of her failure in one of her most impressive periods by Jimmy's exclaiming:

"Oh, Miss Laura, if you cut your nails on Friday, you wont have the toothache."

Certainly her exhortation was wasted, unless the remedy it suggested should prove infallible. If the teacher expects to accomplish anything, he must expect to work. Usually, in the same proportion as we sow, will be the harvest.

It is the general opinion that question-books are a great assistance to the teacher. In learning directly from the Bible, children are apt to commit the words by rote, and have but little conception of the sentiment. One can easily ascertain this by requesting a boy to give the ideas of a verse in his own language. It will usually prove an effectual mode of procuring silence. Some, however, prefer to originate the questions to suit their class. For an able teacher, who will devote sufficient time to the subject, this may be better. The book is a great aid to those of limited time, and as these questions are prepared for different grades of children, almost any class can be suited.

When a class can learn more than the regular lesson, it is well to vary the exercise by letting them commit to memory some hymn appropriate to the subject, or some brief sentiment worth knowing, such as:

"Little attentions, a minute consultation of the wants and wishes, tastes and tempers, of others, — these are the little things that outshine a thousand acts of showy heroism."

By having all commit the same piece, they can recite in concert, and thus occupy but little time. I know a teacher who writes a short story nearly every Sunday to read to her class. This shows the children that their teacher thinks of them during the week, and it pleases them. Every regular lesson should be perfectly learned and recited before any other exercises are taken up. This is essential. Habits of accuracy are important, and after a few trials it will be as easy for the majority to have a perfect as an imperfect recitation.

If possible have the exercises such that all are kept employed, as it secures their attention and keeps them out of mischief.

Do not try to teach too much. It is unnecessary to convert the class into a theological seminary. The great object is the conversion of their souls, not the cultivation of their intellects. The culture is the means, not the end. It is on the practical Christianity of everyday life that they want instruction — to know how to act when a boy steals their sled or pulls their hair, and in all the minor mosquito annoyances of life, which cause even children of a larger growth to forget themselves. As Mr. Beecher remarked:

"There are many men who would make admirable martyrs at the stake, who fall very low over a cup of cold coffee for breakfast."

It is against the everyday sins that the teacher must try to shield his pupils. The chance of their being called on to refute infidel arguments is exceedingly small, but they certainly will be tempted with anger, intemperance, lying and stealing. Guard them against these, and you will do well. After they grow to manhood, living up to these teachings, their lives alone will be argument sufficient for themselves in favor of a God.

"The most convincing argument in favor of Christianity, is the life of a meek and humble disciple of Jesus."

A teacher should not admit any one to his class without the knowledge of the superintendent. The classes must be so arranged as to have those of the same capabilities and tone of mind together, that all may be interested in the same things.

Habits of punctuality must be inculcated, the teacher setting the example. It is very annoying to have teachers and scholars dropping in during the devotional exercises. The teacher's class-book should be kept written up, marking the children exactly what they deserve, and not through mistaken kindness, marking an imperfect recitation with the highest number. Children soon see the injustice, and despise it. I have frequently heard children sneering at teachers for this. They know that on that system a perfect mark means nothing, save that the scholar succeeded in teasing the teacher to write a lie.

The teacher must see that all sing. The effect of Sabbath School music depends much upon the volume of sound. Children are at times a little bashful about singing, and require encouragement. It should be impressed upon them that it is as much their duty to assist in this exercise as to recite their lesson. It is a duty as well as a pleasure. The teacher must see that all the exercises are attended to and rules are complied with.

There is one duty of the teacher, which, though not exactly coming under the subject of lessons and classes, may yet be made a valuable auxiliary to his instructions. Each teacher should occasionally visit his pupils, especially the poorer ones. It will repay a hundred-fold all the trouble it causes. No paymaster is so liberal as God. A very little done for Him or His, He rewards abundantly. Many are the touching stories told of visits upon the poor children. The delight with which the little ones receive their own especial caller; the dignity with which he is introduced to mamma and sisters; the rapidity with which the good woman's apron dusts a chair; the voluminous apologies for, and wonders why, on this particular day the dirt of years has mysteriously appeared in the room, just because "the master" was coming;

the smoothing of the place where once there was a collar — all show how his visit is appreciated. The poor and the lonely know how to appreciate sympathy. Be bright and cheerful. Tuck in a sunbeam here and there, and raise a hearty laugh, where laughter seldom sounds, to cause momentary forgetfulness of the wearying, worrying, sickening poverty around them. Do not tell them they are lost sinners, or even put the question, "What is the state of your soul?" but put a little life and light into the darkened room and sorrow-stricken occupants. Stir them up and encourage them. Remind them of the blessings of life and health which they still enjoy, and show them in what respects they are getting the best in the fight for life. Do not let them stagnate. Don't let them tell their troubles. Listen to their hopes and joys, but do not talk of hard times and rheumatism, and, above all, don't whine. Leave something for them to think of, if it be only a tract—but let it be a cheerful one on the joys of heaven, not on the horrors of hell. Make the visit so bright that they will almost believe that God sent an angel to rejuvenate them. When you return home think it over, balance the account, and see who received the most benefit. See if you have been well paid, and forget it not.

CHAPTER V.

ON MUSIC.

A FEW words as to the music, that apple of contention, which in some churches seems to be productive of more discord than harmony. Like a thistle, it is rather a delicate subject to handle. One trembles at the thought of meddling, with this theme, yet it is one of the most important instrumentalities of the Sabbath School. Many Sunday School tunes are mere trash. From a very laudable desire to avoid the ponderous solemnity of Windham and Balerma, we have baptized Trankadillo and Old Dog Tray, and received them into the Sunday School.

Music, to be sprightly and cheerful, need not be flippant. Neither is it indispensable that children's songs should be so very simple. Boys will learn to whistle Dixie about as quickly and correctly as Greenville. Children can learn to sing *anything* in the way of a psalm tune, and it is unfortunate that so much rubbish is inflicted upon them. The most popular tunes are not the simplest in the collection. There are some good tunes in all the books, but sufficient attention has not yet been given to the subject. Children's music is in about the same stage of advancement that children's story books were seventy years ago. I do not mean to condemn any particular books, for all are good in their way, and of very great assistance. They are pioneers in the right direction, and are constantly improving. I wish but to call the attention of our able and popular composers to the field open for a really superior work.

I do not think it necessarily wrong to use secular tunes re-arranged, but if equally good ones can be obtained, without such associations, it will be preferable. Select first our good tunes already tested, and then, if better cannot be written, apply to the ballads.

Every school should have an able precentor, a good musician, with a strong, decided voice. If possible, have a good melodeon, or if the school is held in the church where there is an organ, use that. Do not feel that it is too much bother. Do not let the children see that you are getting along with as little trouble as possible, but let them feel that every exertion is made for them. If the organist is unable to attend, some one in the congregation will be found able to play the simple tunes. Some think that children cannot sing with the organ, but the introduction of congregational music has settled that they can. If the organ is used, the precentor should stand before the children and lead their voices in a brisk, decided way. Considerable instruction can be imparted at odd times—for instance, occasionally show them the difference between a musical sound and a scream; tell them how to sing with expression, and how to avoid the nasal twang, etc. If the precentor is a thorough musician, however, he will require no directions on this point. Music is one of the most powerful aids to the Sunday School, and a good precentor is second only to the superintendent.

It is unnecessary to have a very large variety of tunes. If the children sing five each Sabbath, it will be two hundred and sixty a year. They can sing the same as often as once a month, if they are good ones, thus requiring but about twenty-two tunes for the year. Children prefer to sing often the pretty tunes that they know *well*, to having a variety of half learned pieces. Twenty-five are about as many as most schools can remember, for as new ones are added, old ones are lost.

It is well for the precentor to select a dozen or fifteen of the best voices, and meet them occasionally to give them instruction. Let them be the choir, and on festal occasions have a prominent seat to lead the music. Teach new pieces to them first, and it will aid the school greatly in learning them. At the Sunday School concerts let them sit in the choir-seats, and sing the solos, while the school joins in the chorus, which will form a pretty effect, and give a variety.

The whole school should occasionally meet to practice new tunes, at which times some serviceable instruction should be given them, principally in the management of their voices, rather than in the science of music.

I think children prefer to sing two or three verses *often*, rather than to sing a less number of tunes with an increase of stanzas. It is also well to practice singing before the opening of school, that the children may come early, and may find employment as soon as they arrive. The best way to keep them out of mischief is, to give them something to do.

"It is good enough for children," is a common saying. But think not so of them — the very elect of God; naturally so loving and loveable, so pure and simple, that art can find no better model for the angels; who are almost holy until contaminated by men. Think not so to treat those whom Christ has especially welcomed near him, taken upon his knee, and set as an example for all men. Think rather that nothing is too good for children, no labor too great to shield them, no sacrifice too costly to save them. Let choicest music, penned by the ablest of masters, lend her refinement to purify the heart; let art wield her pencil and brush with enthusiasm, to cultivate a pure and delicate taste. Let gold be lavished upon the noblest work that gold knows how to perform, and men and women bring their experience, culture and time, to guide and direct the neglected and forgotten children.

CHAPTER VI.

ON LIBRARIES.

DR. BELLAMY is said once to have spoken as follows:

"When men go fishing for trout, they take a light tapering pole, with a fine silken line attached, and a sharp hook with a sweet morsel of worm on the end. They noiselessly drop the line on the water, and let it float to the fish, who nibbles, and by a slight twitch is landed safely on the bank.

"But when some men go fishing for souls, they tie a cable on to a stick of timber, and an anchor is the hook. On it a great junk of bait is stuck, and with this pondrous machine grasped in both hands, they walk up and down, thrashing the water, and bellowing at the top of their voices, 'Bite, or be damned.'"

There is much of truth in the idea that more skill might be employed in enticing people to accept salvation. Both in the church and the Sunday School, he is usually the most successful angler who pays the most attention to the minutiæ of his tackle, and exercises the greatest skill in throwing his hook. To continue the metaphor, the library is the bait in most schools to draw in the scholars, and, as in angling, much depends on the nature of the attraction. The books must be interesting and entertaining. The more instruction, both religious and general, that can be introduced in them the better. They must differ in character according to the class of pupils.

Some statistics have recently been given concerning the factory operatives in Manchester, England. Among those who had been placed in the poor house and various asylums, fifty-five per cent. were familiar with the histories of Jack Ketch, Dick Turpin, and that class of notorieties, while about the same number were utterly ignorant of the *name* of our Saviour. While we can proudly say that no such statistics could be given by any institution in our country, yet there is a degree of popular ignorance far beyond what most people imagine.

Of course it is often no use to present a volume of "Religious Tracts" to such persons. They will prefer to read the Sunday papers. For them, books of a lively, exciting nature, with some moral, inculcating temperance, virtue, honesty, etc., should be provided, as they will be more likely to read them, and therefore to receive benefit. It is useless to put in ordinary Sunday School libraries such works as Doddridge's Rise and Progress, and Baxter's Saint's Rest. I have frequently seen them, and always they were in an excellent state of preservation, and invariably to be found in their place. Some Schools provide them for the teachers, but generally teachers desire more entertaining works as well as the children. Occasionally a few individuals may be found who will read such books, but as they can be obtained elsewhere, it is probably not wise to invest much money in them for the school. The Sunday School must have the books of the age, and not old musty works, valuable in their time, and not to be despised now, but without the necessary sparkle for children's palates. There are many such "standard" works, which every one praises, many own, and few read.* We treat them as Sterne

*I would not be understood as attempting to cast odium on these works. There are still found a few young people who read them with delight and profit. One of our most eminent living authoresses remarked that there were no books she more eagerly devoured, when a child. Such cases, however, are exceptional, and it is hardly worth while to provide for them.

says we do great men, "learn their titles and then brag of their acquaintance."

The question is often raised as to whether any books should be placed in the library which are not usually deemed devotional in their character. My experience has led me to advise great liberality in the selection of libraries, particularly those for ordinary city schools. One object of the library is to provide wholesome enjoyment for the children during the week, to keep them out of the streets, and at the same time to convey some useful information. If a book will accomplish this, and is of a high moral character, even though it may not be strictly devotional in its teachings, I would admit it. The good it will do during the week in raising the standard of honor and morality, will more than counterbalance the possibility of any *harm* its reading on Sunday may occasion.

Some years ago, my father was the pastor of

the Congregational Church on the island of Nantucket. It was customary for the church to place on every whale-ship leaving the island, a library for the use of the crew. "The Evangelical Family Library," published by the American Tract Society, was selected, and it looked finely in the annual report of the Society to state, "We have placed fifty sets of the Evangelical Family Library on whale-ships during the past year," and a nice little speech could be made about the old fathers of the church preaching to the sailors when tossed upon the mighty deep, etc., etc.

The captain on the first Sunday out would bring the books on deck and tell the sailors to help themselves. With awkward hands they would open a volume to "The Call to the Unconverted," and slowly spell out a page, and then, laying down the book for a fresh quid of tobacco, would forget to resume it. The books would return almost untouched, glued together with the damp and brine gathered by a four years' cruise.

It was deemed best to cast aside these books and send in their place "Sargent's Temperance Tales." They were read and re-read, until leaves and covers obtained a divorce. None ever reached Nantucket again. Captains have stated that two ships meeting in the cold fishing regions of the North, a boat from one would board the other, and almost the first question would be, "Have you any of Sargent's books to spare?" They would circulate from ship to ship as long as a story could be found complete.

The popular newspapers of the present day, containing the exciting stories of "The Bloody Tomahawk, a tale of love, beauty, and daring," are accessible to the poorest. Children find such trash under their eyes continually, and will read it unless something as entertaining is provided. The Sunday School has to compete with it, and it will not answer to furnish old sermons, flavored with a century's bottling. The Sunday School Societies have noticed and acted on this. They have generally given a good set of books, without which it would be difficult to furnish a Sunday school library. Still, many of the books are but little novelettes with morals dropped in here and there — which the children always skip. They are very good and highly moral, only they convey scarcely any useful information. I deem a good child's history, giving real practical instruction, in a readable manner, of higher *moral and religious tendency*, than a sentimental memoir of a good little girl who never did any thing wrong, and who consequently, was cut off from her sinful fellow-creatures at the early age of ten. We want more books to teach us how to *live* in a strong, healthy, moral manner as a preparation to learning how to die.

I would have all of Harpers' story books, many of Miss Edgeworth's works, some of Peter Parley's, Harpers' Abbott's Histories, and many such works not usually deemed entirely religious. This would be an expensive library, as the books would be read, and consequently would not last so long. It would, however, be a *working* library, and accomplish its purpose.

But do not hold me responsible for these opinions unless you link with them the following: Each teacher should glance at every book he gives to his pupils that he may know its character. A book that would be well for one scholar to read, would be unadvisible for another. One child dislikes reading, and is full of fire and steam, and is playing and fighting continually. Give him almost anything to create an interest in books. Lend him a Robinson Crusoe kind of book. Another has had his head turned by sentimental love stories.

Try to turn him back with an exciting history which will teach him something manly and noble. Another is in such a state of mind that, with careful management he may be led to the Saviour. Give him books tending directly that way; of a devotional character, yet interesting and full of life. A girl will often require a different book from a boy. In the present organization of society the one is the passive and the other the active. The girl must be taught to endure, the boy to act. Age will vary the requirements, and a teacher must not feel that every book in the library is suitable for every scholar. It is putting an undue responsibility on the library committee. It is well frequently to question the pupils on the books they have read, to judge of the influence on their minds.

It has usually been deemed unprofitable to have libraries for the lower class of Mission Schools, as the transient members will take books, and when they disappear the books will accompany them. In my own school, (one of this character) I had opposed a library, until a teacher suggested that merely the members of the "Legion of Honor,"* should have access to the library. They being regular attendants, the loss of books would not be very serious, and the privileges of the library would be an additional stimulant for the children to join the "Legion." The plan works well, and exerts a great power over the pupils. If they misbehave, they lose their books for the month.

The best method of preserving the books has puzzled the librarians exceedingly. The Sunday School has been a very efficient colporter in circulating books of a good class throughout the country. It is impossible to devise any plan which will prevent all loss.

*The "Legion of Honor" is described in chapter 8. *Discipline and Incentives.*

The following is an economical method for a large school, and on the whole works the best that I have yet seen.

In the first place have two boards painted as follows:

To 100.		To 200.	
1	2	1	2
3	4	3	4
and	so on	and	so on
to	100	to	200

There should be as many columns of one hundred numbers each as may be required. In the centre of each number there should be a hook or brad. One board should have as many numbers as there are pupils in the school, and the other as many as there are books in the library. On the hooks of the *library board*, there should be round pieces of tin, with a hole punched in them to hang by. These tins must have numbers stamped on them corresponding with their numbers on the board.

Each scholar has a number by which he is designated instead of a name. For instance, James Fox is numbered 36. He desires book No. 48, which is given him, and the librarian removes the tin check from No. 48 on the library board, and places it on No. 36 on the scholars' board. This shows that boy No. 36 has volume No. 48. The next Sunday No. 36 desires another book, but forgets to return the one he already has. The librarian glances at his number, and seeing it covered, refuses to supply the volume until No. 48 is returned. By this method the librarian keeps the whole record and the teacher has no trouble.

The numbers on the board should be arranged in double columns of one hundred, as in the diagram, with the odd numbers on the left, and even on the right, for ease in finding a given number. By having them in columns of one hundred, it is unneccesary to repeat the third figure, and therefore larger figures can be painted in the same space. The boards might be made cheaply, by cutting the numbers from paper and pasting them on, afterwards varnishing the whole to render them secure, or by writing them on a painted board, with a coarse pen.

In calling for the books, the teachers will write on a small strip of paper as follows:

Class No. 16.

36	48, 210, 8, 5, 12.
214	24, 19, 27, 153, 440.

The left hand figures tell what scholar to charge the books to, and those on the right show that he desires one of the five volumes selected. Several are designated, so that if some are out, one can pretty surely be found in.

In returning the books, a similar paper should be sent, only instead of the five numbers to the right, there should be only the number of the book returned. The librarian will compare the returned books and the statement, and if correct, remove the check from No. 36, scholars' board, and replace it on 48' library board.

For very small schools all this machinery is unnecessary, but where there are over a hundred and fifty pupils, this method is the easiest, safest, and best.

The Sunday school Union have prepared another plan as follows: A large card is printed in blank, thus:

Teacher's Name.—JOHN NOBLE.						Class No. 6.
Pupil's Name.	Date. Feb. 9.	Date.	Date.	Date.	Date.	Date.
J. Fox..................	36 14 48					
W. True..................	28 19 13					
Etc.						

The scholars select three or four numbers of the books they desire, and write them on the card as in the diagram. The librarian selects the first one that is in, and draws his pencil through the other figures, so the one left untouched is the one charged to the scholar. The *theory* is, that the teacher will copy this number into the class-book and see that it is returned, but the *practice* is to take no further notice of it. The card soon becomes thoroughly covered with pencil marks, and the record is lost in the mass of carbon. In the board plan the check can hang on the scholars' number as many months as the book may be out.

A third plan shown me by a librarian, which is successful in small schools, is for the librarian to have the names of the scholars arranged in classes, and written on a large stiff card, as follows:

	JANUARY.			
	4	11	18	25
Class 1.—John Bagshaw, . .	33	36		
Andrew Clark, &c.	42	90		
Class 2.—William Mack, . .	4	18		
Michael Dorsey, &c.	28	17		

As the books are distributed, they can be charged on the card, and crossed when returned. A glance will show whether the last book is restored. The card should be large, to allow a plenty of room for figures, and to enable the librarian to hold it while marking the numbers. A fresh card should be prepared monthly, and the outstanding books transferred. If the card is retained long, the pencil marks will become rubbed and confused. Where there are more than ten classes, there should be two cards, so that an assistant librarian can be employed.

There should be a printed catalogue of the books, with their numbers, from which the children, under the guidance of their teacher, can select. Of course, frequently, they will be dissatisfied with their choice, but it must be a rule that no book can be exchanged, or the hour will be occupied in suiting them. If the book is morally unsuitable, the teacher must manage to have it changed, even breaking the rule, though if he has an appropriate one at his own house, it would be better to lend it to the scholar in place of the library book.

When the Sunday School is held in the body of the church, the library can be placed at the end of one of the galleries. There it is out of the way, and the movements of the librarians will not attract the attention of the scholars from their lessons.

In following the plans suggested in this chapter, some money will be required, which almost always seems to be grudged the Sunday School. Usually the unnecessary loss of books in an ill-regulated library is much more than will serve to provide the necessary safeguards, yet we often find churches possessed of such "great hunks of wisdom," that they often approve of this mode of economizing.

When boys do not fancy a book, in order to persuade the teacher to change it, they will often falsely profess to have read it. It is so common a lie that they hardly deem it wrong. It is like the ladies' "not at home." Boys who are commonly truthful will commit this sin.

If a book has been out three weeks, the librarian should write the fact on a slip of paper and hand it to the teacher, who should see that it is returned. If the book is lost, or the pupil sick, he should report the fact to the librarian. It will also be stated in the teacher's monthly report to the superintendent, as explained in Chapter IX.

The library must be under the charge of a smart, active, business man. Considerable ability and labor is required to keep the books of a large school in proper order. The books should all be covered with heavy brown paper, and the Sunday School label pasted on the outside cover as well as the inside, or many books will creep into other libraries. The librarian must be a man of good nature, and patience, for both will be considerably taxed. A Sunday School to be successful, should have three enterprising, energetic, hard-working men — a superintendent, a precentor, and a librarian. With these, any school can be made to run smoothly and efficiently. Not a little of its success depends upon the good arrangement and management of the librarian.

CHAPTER VII.

MISSIONARY SUNDAYS AND MONTHLY CONCERTS.

IT is customary in many Sunday Schools to observe the first Sunday in the month as "Missionary Sunday." In the wealthier schools, the children contribute some money for the support of a missionary, who usually writes a letter to them every month in return. This letter is read to the school, from which circumstance the name of Missionary Sunday is acquired. A contribution is taken up for missionary purposes, and speeches, singing, etc., occupy the time usually devoted to the lessons.

Many schools have also, on the evening of the second Sabbath in the month, a special service, usually held in the church, where the parents and friends are present with the children. The exercises are similar to those of the Missionary Sunday, only no particular reference is made to the missionary field.

I think it is unwise to have both these services. Where the evening service can be held, the usual lessons should proceed in the day-school regularly from Sabbath to Sabbath. Any interruption to the ordinary course of instruction has an injurious influence. If the services are not entertaining, the time is lost. If they are, the children on the next Sunday will be restless, and comparing the two sessions.

If the evening service is held, it is an extra affair, and will be regarded as such. The children's services should be much earlier than those for adults, so as not to keep them up late. If they commence at half past six, and continue an hour and a half, it will not injure the health of the children, coming as they do but once a month. Therefore, I very much prefer merging the Missionary Sunday into the Sunday School Concert, and bringing the whole force to bear on making it a grand occasion.

It is a considerable tax to secure first-class speakers for two consecutive Sundays. There must be several, as the children demand a variety. Also the children prefer the evening service, if for nothing else, the novelty of sitting up late. There are many children who would agree with Sammy, when he complained that —

"My mother always makes me go to bed before I get tired, and get up before I am rested."

The brightly-lighted, crowded house; the organ playing just the same as for "grown folks," and the presence of friends and relatives, all give them enthusiastic delight, and put them in a humor to be pleased with anything. They will take part with great earnestness and zeal. I have often known boys who were too proud to take any active part in the Missionary meeting, to be so roused by the enthusiasm of the evening concert, as to place themselves in prominent positions to show that they were connected with the school.

The missionary news can be as well communicated then as at any time, and many adults being present, the collection is somewhat increased. Not the least advantage, is the fact that this plan keeps the school more directly in the notice of the church. The progress, state, and requirements of the school are seen, and more interest in its prosperity, is inspired.

In a Mission School, it is peculiarly advisable to *especially invite* parents and friends of the pupils to be present at these general meetings. Many will attend them who would not enter a church, and much good may be done.

Attention should be given to the subject of the charities of children. It is very useful to collect the little offerings from hundreds of Sunday Schools for the support of some missionary cause. But is this course, on the whole, the most beneficial to the pupils, and, in the end, to the cause of missions? The primary object of the children's contributions is to foster benevolence, and that course should be pursued which will most clearly teach them the nature and habit of true charity. Giving is not always charity.

> "His lavished stores speak not the generous mind,
> But the disease of giving."

The contribution is taken, and sent off in a manner utterly incomprehensible to the younger children. After a while, in some cases, a letter is received from a missionary, who, in language totally beyond children's intellect, tells what good the cash has accomplished. It seems to me that pains should be taken to let the children see more clearly the relation between the act of giving and the consequent benefit to the giver. The benefit may be merely the satisfaction derived from a consciousness of having done good, but still it is a direct and consequent result of the charity. We must cultivate in them a taste for charity, and let them see that they can derive more personal gratification by doing good with their pennies, than by spending them for candy.

A noble Sunday School in Brooklyn was having a new chapel erected for its use. It is stated that the superintendent (also the chief contributor of the funds,) made a calculation of what each brick would cost, and announced that each scholar might present a brick to the building by paying two cents. Those who gave a certain number received a certificate. Almost every child gave a brick, and many gave a cart-load each. Thus they saw in the chapel the direct result of their generosity, and tasted the pleasure of giving. By purchasing the brick, they saw exactly how their coppers were invested, and the walls were a standing monument to them. They possessed an ownership in the building which prevented their defacing it, and increased their interest in the school.

All schools should be Mission Schools, admitting the rich and poor alike to their benefits. There are many who are unable to attend for want of proper clothing. Boys, with a very commendable spirit of self-respect, will not go into a school of well-dressed children in their shirt-sleeves. The children of the school should be formed into a "Benevolent Association," and their contributions be used to supply such articles as may be required by the destitute children in the neighborhood, to enable them to attend. This must be

O GLORY
E TO GOD O
LOVE

managed with care, that they may not be taunted as "charity children."

The Lee-Avenue school, in Brooklyn, which is under the direction of Jeremiah Johnson, jr., a name that thousands of children will bless for his liberality and care, and who has established probably the very best working school in America, has provided a lot in the Cemetery of the Evergreens, for those of the school who may die otherwise unprovided with a pleasant resting-place. There it is proposed to erect a suitable monument, which will be a perpetual sermon to the children.

These plans will bring the subject of charity directly home to the children, so that they will understand it, and see its practical working. I have frequently known of gentlemen trying to ascertain from children what they understood by giving to the missionaries. Invariably their only idea was, that they sent the money to the heathen; but why, or for what, was a mystery.

Let the children purchase the music-books, and they will be more carefully handled. Let them purchase something for the school, and if it is only a picture that can be afforded, it will teach a more direct lesson of charity than the ordinary method. Nor will the public charities suffer, for the children will be trained to those habits of giving which will last them during life. Thus the ultimate result will be beneficial in every respect.

Whether this last statement is true or not, every school should first take good care of itself, and keep in good running order. Money is a power not to be despised in doing good. Few schools have too much expended on them, and all that can be raised within themselves, can usually be wisely expended in improving their own means of usefulness. Men are apt to think that they must go out of their way to do good. Many a minister has neglected his own children to preach the Gospel to strangers. So frequently money is given away by schools to missions which had much better be devoted to their own improvement.

The exercises of the monthly concert should be planned exclusively for the pleasure and benefit of the children. No one should be invited to address the meeting merely out of compliment. If a speaker cannot interest the children, he should not address them. Speeches should seldom be over ten minutes in length, and five minntes will be better. This is about as long a time as the children can be induced to listen to any one. Let the singing be frequent, and only two verses at a time.

One very good and common exercise is to have a subject announced to the school: "love," for instance. Then have all, or a certain part, of the children find some text in the Bible relating to love; and at the concert, on being called on by the superintendent, one by one rise and recite the texts they have selected. As a little improvement, the superintendent sometimes prepares a series of written questions and answers. A duplicate of each one he gives to the children, who learn the answers. He then reads the question, "What is God?" A little girl in class 10, who has received that question and prepared the answer, rises and recites, "God is love." "How does God love this world?" Boy in class 4 responds, "God so loved the world that he gave his only begotten Son, etc." This plan incites the children to learn some texts, and many of them are much interested in reciting. Little hymns and dialogues may be learned and repeated by classes and individuals.

Passages of Scripture may be learned by several classes, and repeated in concert.

The proceedings must be conducted briskly. Not a moment's interval should be allowed between one exercise and the next, that the children's attention may not be diverted. Make all the exercises animated, that the children may enjoy them. Haydn was once asked how it was that his music was all so bright and cheerful. He replied:

"I cannot make it otherwise. I write according to the thoughts I feel. When I think upon God, my heart is so full of joy that the notes dance and leap from my pen."

So should all religious exercises, particularly for young persons, be sparkling, that their thoughts of religious matters may be joyous.

The following programme for a concert will explain what I would suggest:

1st.	Singing by the school . .	occupying	4	minutes
2d.	Prayer, concluding with the Lord's Prayer, by the school	"	4	"
3d.	Singing by the School . . .	"	4	"
4th.	Repeating the Ten Commandments in concert	"	4	"
5th.	Reciting Scripture questions . .	"	5	"
6th.	Opening address by a large boy .	"	4	"
7th.	Singing solo by a little girl . .	"	3	"
8th.	Address by an invited guest . .	"	8	"

9th.	Singing; a duet by two girls . .	occupying	4	minutes.
10th.	Reciting Scripture questions . .	"	5	"
11th.	Poetry recited by a very small boy	"	2	"
12th.	Poetry recited by a very small girl	"	2	"
13th.	Singing by the School . . .	"	4	"
14th.	Reciting Scripture questions . .	"	5	"
15th.	Reciting Psalm by two classes in concert	"	5	"
16th.	Address by a gentleman . . .	"	8	"
17th.	Singing solo by choir; chorus by the School	"	5	"
18th.	Address by a gentleman . . .	"	8	"
19th	Singing by the School . . .	"	4	"
20th.	Closing exercises, as in article on the formal exercises of a school. .	"	2	"
	Total.	"	90	"

This is as long a time as it is well to continue the exercises. They must be continually altered, that the children may not tire of them. It will be found much easier to get the children into school than to keep them there regularly. The novelty often attracts children, who will certainly leave when the novelty wears off. You must keep your eyes open for new and popular speakers. If you can make no other change, hang up a large map or picture where it can be plainly seen, and have some one tell a story of a certain place which he points out on the map. A very slight change and oddity gives freshness and life to the exercises. Most of the children understand and are interested more in what they see than in what they hear.

A few weeks since I heard a most admirable Sunday School speech. On the whole it was better adapted to children than any other I have listened to. It was fresh, entertaining, healthy, and to the point. The speaker at one time was alluding to persons shutting their ears, and as a gesture, put his fingers up to his own ears. As I left the church I met a very bright, intelligent little girl of six years.

"Well, Lottie, how did you like the meeting?"

"First-rate, sir; it was real nice."

"Whose speech did you like best?"

"Mr. M.'s, sir; it was the best *I* think."

"What part of the speech did you like best?"

"Oh, I liked it where he put his fingers up to his ears. It was so funny I laughed right out. Oh, Mr. M. is *so* nice."

She had forgotten nearly all the moral, most of the illustrations she could not recall definitely, and only some such significant actions were particularly impressed upon her mind.

I refer to this to show the necessity of having all the exercises extremely simple, and have such a variety that the youngest, who cannot by any possibility comprehend the most of the remarks, may enjoy as it were, the panoramic effect of the scene.

We must remember that while the Sabbath School aims high, and all the exercises are designed to secure the salvation of each child, yet this cannot always be successful. Some persons seem to believe in salvation or nothing —either make the children Christians, or abandon them. But we must strive to make them moralists if nothing more. This is a good work, and even this is hard enough. At first we go to work with zeal, determined to, and believing we can convert them. Soon we begin to feel that we should be satisfied could we see some moral improvement, and finally, losing all confidence in our own power, we despair, and cry to God to take our classes. Then, *sometimes*, we begin to see a litttle improvement. But the true, humble, Christian teacher will have little success compared with the numbers in school, even though God is working with him. It may be that he will grant us success in inspiring morality, when we cannot lead them to Christ. Therefore I would have this point not lost sight of. Strive to make all the exercises and meetings pleasing, not only to those interested in religious truth, but also to those who are utterly careless. Let them be entertained, to cultivate in them a taste for higher and more improving pleasures than street rowdyism.

I cannot conclude this article better than by using the words of the "Country Parson," whose healthy, manly, touching article on the "Sorrows of Childhood" adorns the pages of the March *Atlantic Monthly.*

"Let me say to every reader who has it in his power, directlv or indirectly, to do so, Oh! do what you can to make children happy; oh, seek to give them that great en during blessing of a happy youth. Whatever after life may prove, let there be something bright to look back upon in the horizon of their early time. Let us try to make every little child happy."

CHAPTER VIII.

TO TEACHERS.

WE usually like to do those things that we can do well. Men are able to accomplish a marvellous amount of labor, if they can only feel that they are doing it satisfactorily to themselves; and the consciousness of doing it well, increases its accuracy. But if we are struggling along, not exactly sure whether we are doing right or wrong, it is wearing and disheartening in the extreme. It is not work that kills a man, but worry. Such a one is likened by Mr. Beecher, to "a candle in a hot candlestick, which burns up at one end, and melts down at the other."

Sunday School work will be extremely irksome and tedious, unless you learn *just how to do it.* No matter how monotonous or simple is an occupation, those who can do it better than any one else, usually enjoy it. A singular illustration occurred recently. A lady, who for many years had been in humble circumstances, remarked that she could hardly be happy in heaven, unless she could do her sweeping and dusting. She had become so accustomed to it, and could do it so easily and well, that she enjoyed it.

I knew of a man that could drive nails exquisitely — this is the right word — and appeared to enjoy the practice as keenly as Morphy does his game of chess. One would suppose this to be as monotonous an employment as any, yet his skill in performing it, made it pleasant.

I never knew a teacher who came to his class without suitable preparation, to enjoy teaching; and I never knew one who was always prepared, to dislike it. It is unnecessary to talk about the dignity of the employment, all know it. But whether dignified or not, if you wish to enjoy your labor, do it well. Do not shrink from the work. You are "soldiers of the cross," officers in God's army, and have a heavy responsibility upon you. Make all the preparation you can; do your work as well as you can, and then your responsibility is at an end.

It is unwise to tease a teacher into the school. If he does not come cheerfully, and with a desire for the work, he will accomplish nothing. Some may be of a retiring disposition, distrustful of their own powers, and may need encouragement, but one must enter with his whole heart into anything in which he would prosper.

There are some little matters, the knowledge of which may save you some annoyance. In pleasing children, some almost ludicrous trivialities may turn the balance for or against you. I remember that a teacher in a Mission School found her class growing very large, and finally it became necessary to place some of the children in another class. When the superintendent came to ask them to make the change, they all stoutly refused. At last one secret of her popularity was revealed in one of the little girl's saying:

"Well, our teacher's got the prettiest bonnet in school, and if I can't stay in her class, I'll go home."

Frequently it is thought kinder not to appear among the poor in handsome dresses; but the poor like to see beauty, even though they cannot possess it. When we go to see the Queen of England, we desire to see her in full dress, though we should not attempt to imitate the crown-jewels on our own person. Let youi class see that you take as much care in preparing for them as for "grown folks," and it will soothe their pride.

Do not find fault with any of the school arrangements before your pupils. They will grumble at the library; show them that it is large and good enough for their use. They will insist that the prayers are too long; quiet them if possible. They will dislike the tunes; remind them that as they run in their heads all the week, they cannot be very bad. In short, point out the silver lining to every cloud that may arise. Make the best of circumstances as they are, yet keep on the watch to improve them if you can.

Teach with animation and spirit, though be careful not to speak louder than necessary, as so many talking makes very much noise. Show the children that you are thoroughly awake. There is a contagion in enthusiasm which can easily be extended to children. They dislike ponderous solemnity in manner and prairie-like sameness in matter.

A boy who had visited an exhibition of statuary, was asked how he fancied it.

"Not much," said he, "I never did like stone gals."

Do not be "stone gals," cold and chilling, wrapped up in formality and stiffness, but "condescend to men of low estate." Listen occasionally to the children's stories, and take an interest in their concerns.

Teach by illustration. There is a little work entitled, "Illustrative Teaching," by W. H. Groser, of the London Sunday School Union, which is republished by Randolph, of New-York. It contains many useful hints on this subject worth knowing.

A truth in a mere didactic form is almost sure to be forgotten: but if linked to a fable, a picture, or a good story, the illustration being remembered, the sentiment has to go with it. The skill with which preachers and lecturers introduce appropriate illustrations, often determines their relative success and popularity. Even our Lord, in his addresses, made great use of illustration to fix his truths in the minds of his hearers, by linking them to parables; so the evangelist says, "Without a parable spake he not unto them." The state of society, the mental ignorance of the disciples concerning the mission of Christ, made the relation of our Saviour toward them very much like that of the teacher toward his class.

Illustration is not merely a decorative art. It is a useful, working, an active agent. It will often render clear, passages and truths, which no simplicity of language could otherwise explain to the children. Tupper wrote:

"Precepts and rules are repulsive to a child, but happy illustration winneth him. In vain shalt thou preach of industry and prudence, till he learn of the bee and the ant. Dimly will he think of his soul, till the acorn and chrysalis have taught him. He will fear God in thunder, and worship his loveliness in flowers. And parables shall charm his heart, while doctrines seem dead mystery."

But illustration, to be useful, must be practical and to the point: teaching something in itself. A teacher should not promise the reward of a story if the children will listen to some stale, stupid sermonizing — a lump of sugar after a pill. This disconnects religion from enjoyment, whereas they should be synonymous. The illustrations should be mingled with the truths of the lesson, to give force to them, and to act as chariots to carry away the sentiments. They must all be brought to bear on the one point of the lesson, as the solar system revolves around one common sun — receiving their heat and brilliancy from the one grand truth.

In illustrating to young children the stories may be fuller and fewer, as they delight in details, and their minds act slowly in receiving the point. For older children less detail is required, as they will sooner catch at the conclusion.

Let the illustrations be of a high order, beautiful in themselves, if possible, and worth remembering.

"Always encourage the beautiful, for the useful will encourage itself."

Anything that will tend to raise the standard of thought is a direct step in the direction of godliness. The illustrations should be judiciously distributed throughout the lesson, to keep a uniform interest and attention.

It is well to have the illustrations drawn from the scenes around them, or so connected with familiar things as to have the moral constantly suggested by the sight of them. For instance, in speaking of truthfulness, you tell your class of the boy in Milwaukee, who was flogged to death by a brutal father, because he would not confess an act which he had not commited; who preferred to die rather than tell a falsehood. You speak of the marble monument which the Sunday School children have reared above his remains, and tell them how it resembles a certain monument in the neighboring church-yard. Thus, whenever they see it, they will remember the story and the sentiment it illustrated. Strive to make the rocks and the trees, the common, everyday things of life, all preach to them of virtue and the love of Christ. Teach them to find—

"Sermons in stones, and books in running brooks."

Practice will enable you to secure any number of illustrations. The little incidents of daily occurrence are of interest, if rightly introduced. You find your class restless and inclined to play. You say:

"Why, children, you remind me of something my little black pussy cat did yesterday."

"At the words, "pussy cat," every eye is on yours, and the children cluster around to hear the anecdote. It is unnecessary to make a long story. You merely add:

"Pussy had been asleep all the morning; but just as I sat down to knit some stockings for the soldiers, she woke and jumped up in my lap. I would have let her stay there for I am never cross to my pussy, and never tease her, so that she is very tame. But she wanted to play, and so rolled my ball of yarn out of the basket on to the floor, and then jumped down to play that it was a great big rat which she had caught. Now, how do you think you are like the pussy cat?"

Charley says, "I guess it's cos we bother you."

"I rather think it must be so; for while I am finding the place for the lesson, you commence to frolic like pussy, which disturbs me. Now, while I am finding the lesson, I want you to imagine you are all pussies, and that I am a mouse which you are watching. You must keep very still or mouse will run away. Some time you can come to my house, and then I will play mouse again, and you can try to catch me."

This will attract their attention, put them in good humor, and keep them quiet for a few moments. It is not necessary to have a well planned story, with its introduction, plot, and deducement. Many persons think it is a very serious and laborious work to tell a story, but nothing is more simple. Begin anywhere. For instance:

"Children, I broke the nose off my tea-pot last night."

"Did you! What kind of a tea-pot was it?" says one.

"Was it smashed bad?" says another, and so on. You can interest a class of small children for half an hour, by telling about that broken tea-pot nose. This is the lowest class of illustration, but one can soon improve so as to make the incidents beautiful and instructive.

You will find great assistance by associating with the other teachers, in the teachers' meetings, which shall be held weekly. This is especially necessary in small villages, where there is not much life and novelty. These meetings should be opened with prayer, and any questions relating to the school discussed. Such questions as the following will arise: "The best mode of interesting the church in the Sunday School;" "The best mode of discipline;" "Shall teachers be employed who are not church members?" Let each teacher who has any such question present it, and then the meeting can decide which one to discuss first. Let all present, young and old gentlemen and ladies, express their opinions on the subject. These should be perfectly free, and unbiased by the wishes of others. Many useful hints will thus be acquired, as each question secures the result of the thought and experience of all the meeting.

When there are no questions to discuss, the lesson for the next Sabbath can be looked over, or an especial Bible-class instituted. But the most important element is the social reunion. All should mingle as equals. As far as possible, the forms and stiffening etiquette of society should be suspended.

It is stated that once upon a time a woman's-rights meeting was held, at which no men were admitted. A reporter for a daily paper concealed himself in the hall, in order to present the speeches in the morning edition. But finally the proceeding became too funny even for his professional dignity, and the representative of the press was discovered by his loud peal of laughter. Mrs. Presidentess said:

"Sister Stubbs, will you turn that man out?"

"No, I wont," responded the sister, energetically, "He's never been introduced."

In the teachers' meetings this rigidity of introductions may be modified. For the evening, all should be acquainted, though no one should presume on it to press the acquaintance further, unless it is expressly intimated that it will be agreeable

In a previous chapter I have referred to the teacher's duty of visiting his scholars. Your influence out of school may be considerable. If the Sunday School lesson is on humility, do not illustrate your precepts during the week by being too proud to notice your pupils in their working dress, even though they are taking home a bundle. Rev. Mr. Cecil says:

"My people look at me six days in the week to see what I mean on the Sabbath."

Be particular to greet new comers cordially, and make the first Sunday in the class pleassant. Much will depend on their first impressions.

In one of the lake cities of New York resides a Rev. Dr. L., whose cordial, genial manner has won the heart of every child who has seen him. He never passes one in the street without a bright, kind word. One day a little girl came dancing in high glee to her mother, and exclaimed,

"Oh, mother, what do you think! *I almost met Dr. L!*"

This is the kind of affection you must inspire, if you expect to have much influence. You must be the children's idol.

You must be careful not to teach anything which a conscientious parent disapproves. For instance, since these articles were commenced, I received a letter from a strong temperance lady, who stated that the teacher of her little daughter took her home one Sunday and gave her cake and wine. Such an act can hardly be too severely censured. Respect a parent's scruples highly. Nothing can be taught so valuable as to compensate for a child's contempt for the parent's strict ideas of right and wrong.

In schools which are not sectarian, it is, in my judgment, unwise to teach controverted doctrinal points. There are enough general truths on which all evangelical Christians agree, to afford ample scope for the teachers. Particularly in Mission Schools is it unwise. In Germany and Prussia, the technicalities of Christian sects are prohibited by a special statute from being taught in Sunday Schools.

You must be prepared for a long, hard work, with but little apparent success to encourage you. Often your labors will appear useless, yet do not be discouraged. Not seldom the child you expect least from, and who seems utterly untouched by all your appeals, will unexpectedly show that your labors have not been in vain. Since these articles were commenced, a lady told me that she was utterly discouraged because she could see no good result from her teaching. The very next Sunday her most troublesome boy stopped her after school, and told her in boyish language, that he was an orphan, and in the spring would be bound out to a farmer, and he should like to have Jesus go with him as a friend, just as she had said he would. How should he get him? He is now attending all the religious meetings, and it is to be hoped that he has experienced a change of heart.

The saving of a soul is worth a life-time of labor. Many a faithful missionary and minister has worked during a long life and seen not one gathered in as the fruits of his teaching. I remember a noble and interesting minister, who told a friend that in twenty-eight years' preaching, God had not let him see one redeemed soul that should bless him. Not a week after, he told this friend that he was satisfied and happy, for since the conversation one young man had written to him and called him his earthly saviour. He was content. His life was a success, for he had saved one soul.

I have just heard the following passage from the letter of a young minister, which, without permission, I transcribe, as it exactly expresses the feelings which should actuate the faithful teacher.

"Within the last few weeks my feelings have entirely changed in reference to my duties as a minister. There is more of the Spirit in my heart, and I feel great pleasure in my labors from the thought that I work, not for self, for fame, or for my people, but for Jesus, my Lord and Saviour. I am His minister, not the church's."

With this spirit, and with energy, what teacher could but succeed. We are far too apt to deem it our duty to convert the class. It is a mistake. It is only our duty to *try* to save them.

Teachers are often like boys who plant peach-stones, and then sit down to see them sprout up. The man that buries an acorn seldom sits under the branches of the oak, yet the tree is planted and grows. Teachers must "learn to labor and to wait."

It is obvious that a teacher should have a care not to neglect the spiritual culture of his own children, in his zeal for his class Yet it is by no means a rare error. I know of some earnest teachers, who entrust the culture of their own children almost entirely to others, while they labor patiently for the children of strangers. Indeed the adage that "the minister's son and deacon's daughter, are the worst children in town," too often has proved true.

Act with gentleness and forbearance with the children, and you surely must do good. Converse with each in private on the subject of religion with a spirit of kindness and love.

Kindness opens the heart as the sun does the flower. The flower bathes in the warmth, and the sun dances for joy at the beauty it has caused. So the recipient of sympathy blesses the friend, and the giver is warmed by the fire he has kindled.

CHAPTER IX.

ON DISCIPLINE AND INCENTIVES.

IT is said that so long as one can face a wild beast, and keep his eye fixed upon his, the animal will not venture to attack him. Whether true or not, the will of a person able to stare a growling lion out of countenance, must have great power. To a greater or less degree, all animals have the ability to distinguish instinctively between their master and their servant. Children know whether it is father or mother that is to be obeyed, even before they can call them by name. Discipline is not enforcing order by punishment, but in securing obedience *without* it. He is the better disciplinarian who can accomplish his end solely by force of character and will.

A person may, perhaps, deter a child from committing a specific act, by the threat of a flogging, but this is not at all the principle of discipline. It is to educate a child to avoid doing wrong, first because it is displeasing to its friend, and afterwards from the nobler motive of disliking the sin of the act. Flogging never stimulated the working of this higher nature. A dog is careful not to bite his master, less because he is afraid of a whipping, than because he loves him. Whipping has done incalculable mischief in teaching children to tell falsehoods. It has made ten liars and hypocrites where it has cured one. There is something so barbaric and disgusting in a whipping, that few children have the moral courage to confess a fault which they believe will be so punished.

A proverbial liar was discussing the propriety of corporeal punishment as a means of discipline. "I can remember being whipped only once, and that was for telling the truth," said he.

"It cured you of it, didn't it?" observed a listener.

Corporeal punishment may be very necessary in some few cases, being a kind of dentist's turnkey, to extract sins that every other instrument fails to move; and one should be used about as often as the other. As the world progresses in civilization, the severity of punishment is being changed to a milder yet more even and certain discipline. Even animals are treated better. Rarey enforces as strict and prompt obedience as the old cowhide flourishers ever attained, and all humanity rejoices. The army and navy found that abolishing the lash was almost the abolishing of the cause for its use. South Carolina still retains the "cat," as a State punishment for male and female malefactors of all colors, and we see what the barbarism which has allowed her to retain this savage custom has brought her to. But the world is slowly learning to rule by kindness, to imitate Christ's example, and lead by love, more than by fear.

Not a little has the Sunday School, quietly and unnoticed, contributed to this reform. A few years since, not a district school was without its birch rod and fool's-cap ostentatiously exhibited. Now they are abolished, or put out of sight, to be used on very rare occasions. It was formerly one of the first lessons for a country schoolmaster to learn how to pummel the big boys. To a certain extent this was necessary, as they were accustomed to the same inhuman treatment at home, and would respect only a physical master. Old Samuel Johnson said, "The only way to get Latin into a boy is by flogging it in." Every true man should hate him with a righteous indignation, for the degradation he would inflict on one, "created in the image of God, but little lower than the angels." I remember how my face flushed at the thought, and how my fists would clench as I neglected my Latin verbs to plan a campaign of school-boys against the crusty old great man. I hated him then, and I despise the sentiment now.

A Sunday School teacher asked Tommy who made him, but he could not tell. She asked Willie, who gave the correct answer. She reproved Tommy for his ignorance, and was surprised that he should allow Willie, who was three years younger, to outstrip him in knowledge.

"Pooh!" exclaimed Tommy, "Bill hasn't been made near so long as I, and of course ought to remember better."

So, I have not been so long made a man as to forget how I was influenced as a boy; what boys liked and disliked; how they were influenced by different treatment; and how a pleasant man, with a kind word for all, could manage us as a potter his clay.

The Sunday School is a living example of the power of kindness and love. Without any formal authority over the children, they obey well. Not even able to compel attendance, children are as punctual as it is their natures to be — full as much so, as at day-school. The schools are often established in the most degraded neighborhoods, where the vicious and ignorant are gathered in by hundreds. Very soon they learn the new and wonderful means of discipline, and instinctively obey it. The Mission School enforces as good order as any school, and the children love instead of hate it. The building is as little injured by vandalism as the school-house; and in every respect the obedience is equally good. Certainly, the children learn as much during the hour as during any hour at the day-school. I know not where we can find a more striking example of the beneficial working of Christ's law of love.

I am a firm believer in strict discipline; in securing prompt obedience. No class can be successful which is not under the perfect control of the teacher. But obedience can be secured in a way to let the boys feel that are forced to it by fear of punishment, or they can, by pleasant, good-natured firmness, imagine they have no desire to do wrong. Have a care to avoid all fretfulness, impatience and anger. An exhibition of either, will seriously damage your moral power. Scolding is seldom advisable, as it is rare that telling a boy he is bad will cause him to resolve to be good. Prove to him that he is wrong, and persuade him *to admit it*, and then there is a chance. Keep the boys good-natured if possible, even when punished, and after punishment, do not leave them until you have talked to them, or romped them into good-nature again. If necessary, take them home, and do almost anything to make them leave you with friendly feelings. Three quarters of the benefit of punishment is lost, if it is allowed to rankle in the heart of the offender. Make the child submit, whatever effort may be required, and then pet and caress it into loving you better than ever. Put down the first indications of a rebellion before it has fairly broken out. At all hazards maintain your authority, even though it may be necessary to call in an officer and arrest the offender.

The ground-work of a teacher's power must be in making his class the pleasantest place for the children. He can usually punish them only by a deprivation of enjoyment. Therefore, all sorts of expedients must be devised for giving the class pleasures, so that expulsion will be a real privation. Let him occasionally invite the children to his house, and entertain them with a romp. A cheap excursion now and then will be serviceable, and a visit to a panorama will bind them securely. Continue your authority over them at such times, that they may acquire the habit of obedience. Never let your orders be disobeyed wilfully, in the slightest matter, and having thus to stand up to your directions, be careful that they are exactly right before you give them.

A few weeks since I witnessed a very good example of what I mean. A lady requested her class to repeat a lesson in concert. For some reason one of the boys refused. As this was the first insurrection, it was necessary to make an example of it. After trying in vain to persuade him to do his duty, she told all to lay aside their books and keep perfect silence. She informed the offender that he had publicly insulted her, and that he must make public reparation. It was necessary that all should obey her, and he must either recite the lesson or leave the class. He was to have three minutes to decide whether he would obey or have the superintendent called to place him in another class. Watch in hand, she waited in perfect silence, and at the time asked his decision. He hesitated an instant, and then replied that he would obey. The lesson was recited, and the exercises went on as usual.

The trouble was instantly over, and no other boy would dare to question her authority. At home, he would probably have received a flogging for the same offence, which would have rankled in his breast, and led him to vow that he would thrash his father as soon as he was big enough. Here the punishment was much more severe in some respects, yet not so irritating. The severity of the punishment usually has less influence in deterring from evil than the certainty of its infliction.

One of the best modes of securing obedience,

is by example. A teacher should at once obey all the directions of the superintendent. That is, when the school is told to rise, the teachers should be the first to start. When order is called, a teacher should drop her story or remark immediately, and give attention. Thus your scholars will see that it is not degrading to obey, and insensibly follow the example. I deem this very important.

Do not demand too much. Discretion and order are the fruits of much patient care. Do not attempt to draw the rein too tight at first. Keep it firm, and gradually draw in. After all, boys have to be managed much as trout. If you do not let them run a little now and then, they will snap their lines. Don't let them have any *slack*, but you must let them run.

An admirable and successful superintendent told me that in his Mission School there was as Irish boy, about fourteen years old, whom no one could manage. He was full of fun and steam, and could not possibly resist the temptation to perpetrate a joke, which was sure to upset the gravity of the class, and not unfrequently that of the teachers. The superintendent therefore told him, confidentially, that he had considerable ability, and by study, might make a first-rate teacher. He gave him a class of small boys, and showed him how to conduct it. Pat put all his soul and energy into the work. He would prowl the streets after boys who did not attend any school, and almost drag them in, until he had a large class. He ruled them with a rod of iron, and exacted military obedience, making the little fellows toe the mark exactly. But he was so full of enthusiasm, quaint humor, and tact, that he made them like him, and roused them to work well. On the whole, as far as mere discipline and management is concerned, it was one of the most successful classes in school.

The following plan has received the approval of a teachers' meeting, but I have never seen how it works; yet I have confidence in its operation. Let the superintendent give a notice, with a little flourish and considerable enthusiasm, somewhat as follows:

It is proposed to form a society composed only of the noblest and best members of this school. It will be called the "Legion of Honor," and it will truly be an honor for any one to belong to it. It is in the power of any scholar to be appointed, by conforming to these rules:

1. He must have been punctual at each Sunday School for the four weeks before Missionary Sunday.

2. He must have preserved a good deportment in his class, and whenever in church.

3. He must have returned all his library books, save the one taken on Missionary Sunday.

Each teacher will keep a record of these facts, and before the opening exercises on Missionary Sunday, will give the superintendent a list of all in his class who have complied with these rules.

On each Missionary Sunday (or monthly concert) the superintendent will make an honorable mention of them, and as their names are called they will gather around the superintendent's desk. The superintendent, or some one whom he will invite, will address them a few words of congratulation, and declare them, for one month, members of the LEGION OF HONOR.

The members being all faithful and trustworthy, not requiring watching by their teachers, as a mark of confidence in them, they will be ushered into the front seats reserved for them. They will set an example of good manners and polite deportment worthy of the high distinction they have received.

A list of the members will be posted in the vestibule of the church. At all celebrations and festivals the "Legion of Honor" will receive with especial respect, the positions of trust and distinction. They are to feel that they are honored for their virtues, and any rudeness or unbecoming behavior will be much worse, coming from them, than from those who are not members, and will disgrace not only the individuals but the school.

The success of this plan will depend entirely upon how it is managed. It must be treated as a grand affair, and carried through with enthusiasm. At first the boys will laugh at it, but after one or two speakers have referred to it in glowing terms, and all see the ceremony, etc., they will conclude that it is something after all. Teachers must be honest in their reports, or it will kill the whole affair.

It is well to have the membership last but

one month, so that the scholars can have the pleasure of hearing the names frequently called. Otherwise they will become accustomed to the society and backslide.

It will also be necessary to continually devise novelties for the Legion, to keep up the interest. In my school I only invite these to our festivals and little gatherings. If the children find they obtain more privileges when in the Legion, they are very zealous to join, and soon nearly the whole school will be members. I have known the plan to fail for want of change. Children quickly tire of sameness.

The exercises will occupy some time, but probably the children will be more interested in them than in most of the speeches they will listen to, and as the meeting is expressly for their benefit, anything that pleases them is best.

The superintendent of a large school should

require from the teachers a monthly report, that he may keep the run of affairs. The attendance and character of each pupil comes under his notice, and this fact being known to the scholars, has a very beneficial effect. It is well to have a little form prepared somewhat as follows:

MONTHLY REPORT FOR *FEBRUARY*, 1863.

Teacher—*James Smith.* Present, 3 Sundays. Class, No. 64.

Pupils.	No. of Sundays present.	Books out.	Deport-ment.	Remarks.
A. Brown...	*Four.*	*None.*	*Good.*	
C. Downs..	*First and Third*	*No.* 861	*Hard to manage.*	*Should be changed into a higher class. Has lost book No.* 861.
Etc.				

DIRECTIONS.—If any pupil is sick, please state it. Also, mention whether any one has called; if so, who.

Henry Sims was sick for two weeks. My wife called. He expects to be at school next Sunday.

J. S.

In preparing any forms, have them as simple as possible, that they may occupy but little of the teacher's time in filling up. Indeed, some strips of paper, cut of a uniform size for convenience in handling, and distributed to the teachers, would accomplish the purpose. Still, the printed form saves time and secures accuracy. Most of the information is taken from the teacher's class-book, and can be quickly written.

The superintendent should examine the reports, and occasionally speak to the pupils individually about their marks. Especially if he can praise a scholar, let him do it. Some people are exceedingly afraid about giving any commendation; but more children have been injured by scolding than by flattery.

Sulkiness in a scholar is the most difficult thing for a teacher to manage, and the most trying to the patience. Scolding does not a particle of good. Reasoning is utterly lost, and if ever a whipping is of service, it is here. But a teacher cannot apply that, and therefore, good nature must come into play. Tell the funniest stories you can think of, not directly at the patient, lest it attract attention and rouse his pride to hold out; appear not to notice it, and, if possible, do not do anything to bring it to a climax, where your own dignity will require you to compel the pupil's submission. Get him into a laugh, and all is right. It is better even to sacrifice the whole lesson in telling stories, than to get into a contest. It will spoil the hour for yourself and the class at any rate. Almost always a good romp, with a little tickling and merriment, will shake the sulks out of any boy; and it is vastly better to romp it out than to flog it out. This cannot be conveniently done in the Sunday School, but try a mental romp, with all the fun at your disposal. Don't lecture him while the fit is on, but when it is all over; the next day, perhaps, give him a serious talk. Ten to one, he will express his regrets.

The teacher must work into the affections

of his scholars, that they may rely on him as a friend. Always notice them in the street with a polite cordial bow. Not with a nod, as one would hail an omnibus, but with a pleasant smile, to show you are pleased to see them. Don't be afraid to touch your hat occasionally. Our nation is not particularly noted for its politeness, and this act of courtesy is fast becoming resigned to the "gentlemen of the old school." Our modern contemptuous nods would make the ghost of Chesterfield shudder. A young man in a New-England village, who happens to have habits of refined politeness, is branded with that intensely Yankeefied sobriquet, "stuck up." But politeness is a *power* as well as an accomplishment. Be polite to your class, and they will be so to you. If the boys are large, call them "Mr."; if from twelve to fifteen, call them "Master" John or James. They will laugh at first, but it will please them. Some of these little formalities will enable you to be more familiar in other matters without their presuming on it. In short, practice that politeness "which is a natural, genial, manly deference; with a natural delicacy in dealing with the feelings of others, and without hypocricy, sycophancy, or obtrusion;" a politeness which is always acquired by following the precepts of the Golden Rule.

CHAPTER X.

ON SPEAKING TO CHILDREN.

THE superintendent of a Sunday School was questioning his pupils concerning the addresses made to them during the previous session.

"Children, what did Mr. Phonny tell you this morning?"

No answer was made.

"Can't any one tell me what he said? Susie, can't you remember?"

Susie, a bright little one of seven years, arose, and with one finger in her mouth, bashfully lisped out:

"Pleathe, thir, he talked and he talked, and he thed ath how he loved uth, and he talked — and — and — we all thought he wath a-goin' to thay thumthing, but he din't thay nothing."

This would be a very correct criticism of very many a Sunday School speech — and possibly of some others. There seems to be an idea prevalent that anything will do for children. Speeches are too often vague, indefinite remarks, about being unprepared, little to say, loving children, happy to see them, and then — nothing. This mode of address has become rather old to the children. It is like presenting a Bible to your pastor — a very pretty gift, and appropriate, though another might be more acceptable, as probably he already possesses a copy of the Scriptures.

There is hardly any kind of speaking which demands more originality, and a certain kind of knowledge of human nature, than effective Sunday School addresses. There are comparatively few really telling Sunday School speakers. One reason is, that men often try to speak for effect. They are ashamed to bring themselves down to children's level, forgetting that it is not an inferior character, but merely a different one. We instinctively desire that our friends should be pleased with our remarks, and speak of ours as a fine speech. Many carry this perfectly proper ambition to the extent of speaking for fame, rather than to do good. They therefore try to adapt their remarks to both children and adults, consequently sharing the usual fate of compromisers, displeasing both. A speaker must adapt his remarks entirely to the smaller children, and if successful in interesting them, he will pretty surely entertain the older ones. It is a singular, though a well-known fact, that a first-class speech or book which interests children, will please adults. The Pilgrim's Progress is the usual example cited for this. Interesting to youth, age has read and re-read it with delight. So let the speaker devote his efforts to making a capital children's speech, and if he succeeds, he will be appreciated by adults. He who works merely for fame, seldom secures more than notoriety. He who presses forward in the path of duty, to do good, is very apt to wake up and find himself famous.

Always have one direct practical truth to enforce, and only one. Children can receive but a single idea at a time. All the illustrations must point to it. In the words of another, "illustrate and repeat, simplify and illustrate." The story that strikes the attention of some will not bring the point home to others. Therefore much repetition of the illustrations is necessary, until the subject is made clear and impressed upon the minds of all.

If possible, speak of some special sins which you know the scholars are guilty of. Be definite and practical. Do not merely tell the children to be good, but show them *how* to be good. Take some common fault and show its evil, degradation, and contemptibleness. Use simple language that all can understand.

It is said that a certain theological professor in New-York, whose studies among the dead past, had rather unfitted him for attracting the new, fresh minds of youth, commenced a Sunday School speech as follows:

"My dear little children, I want to give you a summary of the Bible. But, perhaps, my dear little children, you do not know exactly what a summary means. I will tell you. Summary is a — a synonym of synopsis."

Many persons cause their own failure by attempting an argumentative disquisition, with its points, sequences and conclusions. They instinctively feel that if the subject is simple and the words easy, the process of demonstration may be somewhat complicated. Others again, to avoid this fault, fall into stupid truisms expressed very simply. Their remarks are all, "I am glad to see you; I love you:

you must be good children; obey your teachers, and love God."

Children can grasp *one grand idea*, which can be made clear by illustration, while they cannot comprehend a syllogism. Thus very young children can acquire a definite idea of the power and grandeur of God, while they could not at all comprehend the mystery of the Triune Godhead, (though perhaps this inability is not entirely confined to children. Most of us believe while we do not understand.) Children not only can take the one grand idea, but they *require* one, and a good strong one at that, but it must be of such a character as to be illustrated by word-pictures rather than demonstrated by algebraical problems. It must be exhibited, rather than proven to them.

Therefore, do not make assertions at first, which are to be proven and applied at last. They cannot remember the premises. Let the address be a narrative, rather than a syllogism. Children are naturally credulous, and will believe the speaker as readily as they will demonstrative proof. It is unwise, therefore, to attempt to prove a fact to the children except through illustration. If you confuse their minds, all is lost.

Speak in an animated manner, to excite them, and keep them wide awake. Children cannot endure a slow, sleepy, sing-song manner. They want brisk, active life. They are all fire, and must be fought with fire.

A speech must be adapted to the class of scholars you address. If they are from educated families, the remarks may be well polished, and what is termed refined. This class will notice errors of style quicker than those of statement. They are accustomed to believe what is told them, and are therefore more credulous. In the mission gatherings of newsboys and the like, the speech must possess more originality and force, though less polish is necessary. These children are sharp and keen, accustomed to doubt everything, and ever on their guard against fraud. They will detect a weak spot in your statements more readily than the children of luxury, though defects in manner and diction will be disregarded. City and country children will not always understand the same illustrations.

A gentleman informed me that he one day took a class of seven girls in a Mission School in New York city. They were of German parentage, and their ages ranged from fourteen to eighteen years. They were respectably dressed, could read pretty well, and were tolerably intelligent for their station in life. Yet not one in the class knew what a mountain or a wave was. They had lived all their lives in the city, and, though they had read the words frequently, and pronounced them perfectly, they were ignorant of their significations. They had not seen the mountain and wave, and therefore the knoweledge of them had not been acquired. The words being so simple, no teacher had explained them. Sea-side children will often be ignorant concerning backwoods life, and inland children will have no definite idea of a ship. It is well to remember this in adapting illustrations to the understanding of the audience.

In relation to the use of illustrations, I would refer to the chapter entitled "To Teachers."

Speeches should be brief. Length is not strength. Few persons can hold the attention of children for more than ten minutes. Mere attention on their part, or even their assertion that they understand a subject, is not at all reliable. They will often stupidly listen, without interest or not grasping a single idea. Ask them if they comprehend what is said, and they will say "Yes." Question them, and you will say "No."

It is very common to ask children questions during the remarks, to keep their attention. This is a good plan, though in some respects dangerous, unless you are familiar with the school. You may sometimes receive answers not anticipated, which will probably alter the effect you were intending to produce.

A gentleman was addressing the children of a Mission School, in a very solemn manner, and asked them what God first made. A ragged urchin, who had not a due regard for propriety, shouted out, "Cats." Whether the remainder of the address was impressive or not, it is certain that it required serious effort to preserve proper sobriety.

This is not quite so unfortunate as the experiences of a clergyman in Maine, who was opposed to having any mirth in Sunday School. He thought it injurious to all, and unnecessary for the entertainment of the children. He offered to address the school, and show that they could be well entertained seriously. I am credibly assured that the following dialogue ensued:

"Children, I am going to tell you about Peter. Who knows who Peter was?"

No answer was made.

"Cannot any one—those large girls—tell me who Peter was?"

Still no reply.

"Can any little boy or girl in the school tell me who Peter was?"

"I can," said a little fellow in the further corner.

"Ah, that's a good boy. Now you come up on the platform by my side, and stand up in this chair, and tell those large girls who Peter was."

Jimmy did as he was bid, and in the shrill voice of childhood repeated:

> "Peter, Peter pumpkin eater,
> Had a wife and couldn't keep her—"

At this stage he was stopped, but not before the full point was taken by the school, and Mother Goose's poem appreciated.

It is dangerous asking questions of children. They are what we Yankees call "cute," and will often throw an inexperienced speaker into confusion. Still, if one is sure of his audience, or is so ready as to be able easily to turn any *mal à propos* remark to account, it sometimes helps keep their attention to let them do part of the talking.

No person has a right to make a stupid address to children, if he can, by preparation make a good one. Whether it be humorous or solemn, it must be good. "A solemn nothing is as wicked as a witty nothing." Every dry address is a positive injury to them, for mankind are but too ready to connect stupidity with religion. There is usually but little excuse for not interesting children, for, while it may require superior and varied powers to blend instruction with entertainment, to move on children's hearts so as to produce a lasting effect, it is comparatively easy to merely interest them. Almost any one who has read or heard a good story, can retail it to the children so as to please them. If amateur speakers would be willing to be more simple and attempt a less grand affair, they would oftener succeed in interesting the audience. Whenever you see an appropriate story in a paper, cut it out, and put it away for future use. If you hear an anecdote, write down enough to recall it to you. If you will merely tell two or three stories, tending to one moral, and tell them well, your speech will be voted a success, and be very likely to do good. One who would draw from a cask, must fill it. He who would present an effective address, must first prepare it. It can easily be done at odd times otherwise lost — during those spare moments which "are the gold-dust of time."

Usually it is unwise to have the regular lessons of the Sabbath School interfered with by speeches. It is particularly dangerous to allow gentlemen to address the school whose abilities you are unacquainted with. It breaks into and effects the influence of the lesson. Regularity is all-important in dealing with numbers. The superintendent's own judgment must determine when this rule shall be suspended.

Speakers must not count too much on doing a vast deal of good all at once. They must not be disgusted if they cannot move the audience to tears. It is not likely that they will have many dating their conversion from the day of the speaker's maiden effort. Sunday School workers must be willing to labor without any present reward. This is their honor; it is for this that they deserve their credit. They will see but little success, and will often be discouraged.

We have read calculations of the number of pounds weight of lead and iron in battle expended to kill each man, and have been astonished at the quantity wasted—utterly lost. If it takes so much labor to kill a man, what must be required to save him! Think of the number of sermons preached, and the few conversions. What a list of apparently wasted sermons would be exhibited in a calculation of the number delivered to each convert. We must not count on doing much—that is, influencing many. One of our shots may tell, and penetrating some iron-clad heart, compensate for all the useless ones. But our guns are not of heavy calibre, and we are inexperienced artillerists. We will keep up the fire, however, as long we have a round of ammunition left and can reach the enemy. But we must not be disappointed if we merely check his advance. There are many "Merrimac" hearts and but few "Monitors" to meet them. We are to do our work, trusting to Providence for its effect. "We are put here, not to date God's works, but to prepare for their forthcoming."

CHAPTER XI.

THE INFANT CLASS.

THE infant class should be to the Sunday School what the Sunday School is to the church — a preparation for something higher. It is the nursery where gentle encouragement and moral pastime inspire a fondness for religion. But little, save the most simple and general ideas of right and wrong, can be taught. The great ends to be attained are to instil habits of attention, attendance at school, and to provide suitable Sunday entertainment with a very little instruction. I sometimes think the less instruction by means of study, the better — for children's brains are enough stimulated during the week without the pressure of Sunday School. I have never fancied infant phenomenons, as they are apt to ripen into adult imbeciles. Therefore, the class should be but as a Sunday play-room with Sunday amusements. There is a Scotch proverb, that "an ounce of mother is worth a pound of preacher." The teacher must aim to assume the familiar nursery conversation and instruction of a faithful parent. The nearer he can come to this, the more decided will be the success.

The scholars in this department should be from three to six years old, or even older if they cannot read. No one who reads with any degree of fluency should be retained.

First and foremost, make the little ones comfortable. Don't perch them up on high seats where their little legs and feet will stick out straight like a yard-stick across a counter.

If possible, have a separate room for this class, where the seats can be adapted especially for them. The seats should be so inclined that all may be distinctly seen by the teacher, and each pupil have the same seat from week to week. By having them arranged to suit the children, a large number can be accommodated in a very small space. A room sixteen by twenty-four feet, will seat 150 children. Further directions for the arrangement of the Infant Class room, will be found in the chapter on "Sunday School Seats."

We all talk about the importance of ventilation, scold at the universal negligence, and then take but little trouble to remedy the evil. I have been into schools where the air was so foul, that, though I refrained from the expression of my feelings, I fear that I was like the Dutch boy who was whipped because, as his father said, "You tink vun swear joost so loud as you can holler." It is about as hard to inculcate purity in such an atmosphere, as to "do up" laces in Mississippi river water; the more they are soaked, the dirtier they become.

Having made their bodies comfortable, set their minds at ease. Receive every new scholar pleasantly and cordially, and make him feel at home. I had the misfortune once to over-do my suavity. A little girl came in, and I put on my blandest smile to receive her, when she began to cry. I was astonished, and was astounded when she exclaimed to her mother, who brought her:

"Ma! that old ugly man is laughing at me."

I could never make friends with her, and cannot say that her criticism added to my regret when a few weeks after she left the school. This shows the importance of first impressions.

There should be both a gentleman and lady superintendent for a large infant school. The children will require almost the constant personal attention of one, while the other is conducting the exercises. A gentleman and wife, or brother and sister, will work well together.

Where it is feasible, it is pleasanter to have all the school meet in the general room for the opening exercises, as the music is improved by the greater volume of sound. The infant class can sit together, and march out to their own room as soon as the school is opened. Where this cannot be, and there is merely a lady superintendent, some gentleman should be present to conduct the opening devotions. Adults are often present as visitors, and it is extremely disconcerting for a sensitive lady to offer a prayer before them. I have always been opposed to any such publicity of conduct which tends to mar that exquisite modesty and refinement which is the peculiar charm of woman. I have known ladies to refuse to take the infant class, lest they should be subject to this embarrassment.

Where no gentleman can conveniently be spared, let the class with folded hands and bowed heads, repeat the Lord's prayer.

A few verses should be read, and so explained as to convey a distinct and clear idea of their meaning — not necessarily all their meaning, but one clear idea.

A story is told of a worthy but uneducated brother, who was conducting a prayer-meeting. Not having previously prepared himself, he opened the Bible at random and commenced to read. Unfortunately, the chapter contained many hard words, which he blundered over, until finally he was stopped by a huge polysyllable. With perspiration upon his brow, he hastily turned to another place, and said,

"Brethren, we will turn to an easier chapter."

Have a care that the passages you read may be so simple that the children will not be inclined to repeat this brother's remark.

The wisest course of instruction is difficult to determine. Almost any mode becomes stale in time, and it is perplexing to devise a sufficient variety in the programme to keep the exercises fresh. One thing should be remembered — the class is to be considered a Sunday play-room rather than a school. American children have enough stimulus six days of the week. Sunday must be a day of rest. Any study or instruction which can be pursued without violating this theory is allowable, but do not excite the little ones so as to put their brains into a ferment.

The greater part of the exercises will be composed of music, to aid in which a small melodeon will be a great acquisition. The children require no books, as they sing only familiar tunes. Sing one or two verses every five or ten minutes, and have the words so simple that all can understand them. They need not be especially devotional in their character, if they only inculcate the great commandments on which "hang the law and the prophets."

One of the most successful infant class teachers in New-York, puts almost everything into rhyme, and sings it, composing the words on the spot, adapting them to some familiar tune. For instance, a boy is restless, and finally manages to tumble off the seat, disturbing the whole school. Instead of administering a scolding, or applying the popular punishment of sitting the culprit *down hard*, he scribbles off the following:

Johnny, keep upon the seat,
And do not tumble off,
For if you do, most truly you
Will make the children laugh.

(The reader is informed that this is the author's first and only poem in print, therefore there is no danger of a new volume of fugitive pieces.)

The children sing it over two or three times, laugh at it, and are careful for the rest of the day.

The teacher must remember such young children cannot sit still for an hour. If the benches are so that the little ones can seat themselves, and the aisles are conveniently arranged, it is well to let them march around once or twice during the session, to rest them, they singing some lively tune. A little practice in this way will have a good effect in teaching them to move out of meetings without crowding and confusion. All these little things are worth knowing, and they are not, for them, improper Sunday employments.

It is well to let the children learn verses of Scripture during the week, to recite in school. Care should be exercised not to stimulate those whose brains are already over-excited, but to repress those, while spurring on the indolent. Have each child who recites rise and speak in a distinct voice. Insist upon this. Have a word of commendation for those who do well, *or try to do well*, while those who will not exert themselves pass over in silence. The thirst for praise will soon lead them to reform. After every few answers make some very brief remarks, to keep the attention of the school, or ask them all to repeat a good text in concert, or ask some question you are sure they can answer, or tell a story which the text suggests. These remarks must be very brief, but a word or two will keep the attention. For instance, Eddie Kellogg says, "little children love one another." You say:

"Children, do you hear that? Christ says, 'love one another.' I knew a boy once who recited his verses in Sunday School, and as soon as he got into the street he pulled off a boy's cap and threw it over the fence. Was this 'loving one another?' No, of course not. Now it is just these teasing things that Christ Jesus tells you not to do. Will you remember this? Now, Willie, what good thing have you to tell us?"

"Remember the Sabbath day to keep it holy."

"Oh yes! that's very good. I am going to talk to you about that some day. Johnny, have you as good a text as Willie?"

Thus, for the sake of hearing what you have to say, they will listen to the recitations. Generally children prefer to recite themselves rather than to hear others, but they are always ready to listen to stories from an adult.

It is unnecessary to have every child recite its verse every Sunday. Go as far as you can, and begin next week where you left off. When the time to close arrives, tell them you are very sorry that more could not recite, but if they will all come early next Sunday you will try to commence sooner, so that more can repeat their verses.

Picture teaching will also be found exceedingly effective. The pictures should be large and well defined, so that all can easily see them. Show not more than one each session, lest the scholars become satiated. Explain the scene elaborately, with as much detail and incidental anecdote as possible. So successful is this course of instruction, that the Sunday School Union have issued a sort of panorama of pictures, so contrived that they can be unrolled one at a time. It is an excellent contrivance.

At a recent lecture, Mr. R. G. Pardee, of New-York, gave some very good advice in regard to teaching the infant class. Healthy children abhor quietude. Perpetual motion is their normal state. All instruction should be conducted in accordance with this law, and suitable exercise should accompany all study, or it will be irksome to them.

For instance, in reading the Bible, it will be well to select such passages as Psalm cxv., verse 4: "Their idols are silver and gold, the work of men's hands. They have mouths, but they speak not; eyes have they but they see not; they have ears but they hear not; noses have they, but they smell not," etc.

At the word eyes, let the children all touch their eyes; at the word ears, touch their own; at the word God, point above, and so on. This will entertain them, keep their attention, and they will learn the passage very quickly.

There are some little books published with acting songs, which are very useful. As long as you can keep up a variety of *action* among the children, so long the exercises will not become irksome to them. I mean, of course, during a reasonable time.

Mr. Pardee thinks that nearly all that is *told* very small children is utterly lost. We can hardly realize how few words they understand. The first few years they learn almost entirely by sight, and therefore we must work through this faculty. He mentioned a school where they had a number of plaster casts, of various subjects. Among others there was one of a dog. He inquired its use.

"Why," said the superintendent, "that is one of my most useful sermons. That is Fido, or the faithful. I illustrate the whole nature of obedience, fidelity, love to his master, etc., by Fido's character. He preaches such sermons to their young minds, as I am unable to. The children will often understand a story about this dog, which they can see, when they would hardly grasp a single idea without having the tangible object before them. There you see a pair of doves, with their bills touching each other — not very beautiful or natural, but very useful. I have stopped all pushing and punching among the scholars, with those doves. Their object is to teach love and kindness to each other."

I am not in favor of giving out library

books to children who cannot read. Many will be lost. Those which are preserved will cause parents the trouble of looking after them. The parents, not the children, will return them. The children will be obliged to have some one read to them, if the books are used at all, and parents or friends who will take this trouble, will, in this day of cheap publications, obtain books in other ways. As a general rule, I have found parents opposed to their young children taking books. When any parent especially desires a book, it can be supplied from the general library. Much time will be spent in supplying the books, and, in vulgar parlance, they are "more bother than they are worth."

If the school can afford it, it will be well to give the children picture-cards or papers. One pretty card or paper a month, as a gift, will be more prized than a volume loaned.

There is no position in the Sunday School

more pleasant than the superintendence of the infant class, for one who is successful. The children are at just the age when they are easily managed, and full of childish originality. A volume might be filled with touching and amusing incidents of such children.

Last winter, a little boy who was deaf, and talked only as he did when he was three years old, with the peculiar devotional character so frequently found in such unfortunates, had been praying every night for snow. At last it came. As soon as he saw it, he rushed into his sister's room, shouting:

"I so very happy indeed. All up in the sky work so very hard. Papa in the sky, (his name for God) brother John, little sister, all work so very hard indeed all night, making snow for Gorham," and he fell on his knees exclaiming, "Thank you, Papa in the sky, thank you for snow."

CHAPTER XII.

THE BIBLE CLASS.

COLERIDGE once remarked that of all vices, ad-vice was the worse. Certainly it is easier to proffer advice than to profit by; to tell how to act, than to accomplish one's own plans. It is not with a spirit of fault-finding that I speak of the room for improvement in the Bible-Classes. They are generally well conducted. I merely detail the hints I have gathered in visiting many schools, and suggesting such additional things as may tend to make the duties of the Bible-class teacher easier and more successful. A teacher, however, who merely follows the plans "laid down in the books," will be as often defeated as would a general of like habits. Those are successful who can originate new manœuvres for new exigencies, who have, what we term, "genius," to step out of the beaten track, *where a new is better*, and lead their class through fresh scenes. Yet a care must be exercised not to carry novelty so far as to forget the grand object of the labors, viz.: to save souls.

That many of our Sunday Schools are sadly lacking in adult Bible-classes, is not the result of neglect deserving censure. Probably no subject connected with the school has received more thought or has been surrounded with more difficulties. It is exceedingly important that persons from fourteen to twenty years of age, should be retained in school, yet how to keep a hold on them is perplexing. Just at the most critical portion of their lives, a feeling of pride leads them to deem the school a mere children's affair, unsuitable for young men and young ladies. It is of no use openly to combat this pride, for opposition only develops it.

"He who wrestles with us, strengthens our muscles."

We can only ignore it, work around it, and undermine it. Frequently where a person has one set, determined prejudice, he is so intent on watching for a direct attack on his hobby, that he will not notice an attempt to outflank him, and may be bound hand and foot by an approach in any direction save over that particular rampart of pride.

Dr. Todd, in his most admirable work, entitled the "Sabbath School Teacher," proposes to have every scholar, who leaves the school, given a certificate of honorable dismission. By this means the superintendent can usually learn who are intending to leave,. and why. Some management and care, will ordinarily induce those to remain, who only leave on account of age. I think this plan feasible.

Sometimes adults can be induced to join a Bible class if it is held separate from the Sunday School; where no one can confound them with the "children." It is better to go directly forward without this circumlocution where we can; but he who attempts, under all circumstances, to "walk straight onward, turning neither to the right nor the left," will be likely to experience an unpleasant collision. We must manœuvre to win souls if we cannot save them otherwise.

A friend was trout-fishing on the sides of "Old Saddleback," a mountain in the interior of Maine, a hundred miles from the coast. Supposing himself ten miles from any village, and half as far from a house, he was surprised by hearing the blows of an ax. Soon he came to a small clearing, where the proprietor of the ax surveyed him with some curiosity.

"Hallo, stranger!" said he.

"How are you, sir?"

"Well, now, stranger, where be ye from?"

"I'm from New-York."

"From New-York! Why, I should think you'd hate to live so fur off."

Now, even though we may not believe that we live directly on the universal hub, still we all have our pet prejudices and foolish pride, which no argument can reason out of us. There is no use of telling a boy how foolish it is to be ashamed to go to Sunday School. Humor his pride for a while, and let him attend what you call a "Bible History Circle." As soon as he becomes interested, his pride on that point will evaporate.

In selecting a teacher, not always are the most learned the best adapted to impart knowledge to the class. I sometimes think that a person but a few degrees above the class in culture—if a growing man—is about as likely to be successful as any, for the reason that, being near their own standard, he is interested in about the same things as his pupils, and understands their calibre. He must have some tact in managing to avoid the appearance of a school-master's authority, so as not to frighten them away by the fancy that they are treated like children. He must understand what the "Country Parson" calls the "Art of putting things."

In gathering a Bible Class, be careful, as far as possible, to have all of the same general turn of mind together—that is, those who can all be interested in the same subject. Some are mathematical and precise, wishing the doctrines of the Gospels demonstrated. They are lovers of creeds and denominationalism, placing much importance on the literal observance of a literal translation. They delight, so to speak, in the exquisite mechanism of the Gospel. They admire the symmetrical order of the "plan of salvation," and are never tired of examining and discussing its completeness.

Others go to the opposite extreme, and while they admit that some attention to creeds and doctrines is necessary, yet they are not to them pleasing studies. They are as dry husks. The life and character of Christ, his promises of love and assurances of care, supply food for their minds. They are emotional, and desire to be affected through the heart rather than the intellect. Perhaps these exhibitions of truth produce similar effects in minds differently constituted: the one influenced by demonstration, and the other by illustration.

Whether the ultimate effect in the two dispositions is or is not the same, the modes of operating are so antagonistic that they cannot be blended. It would not be well to unite in a select social circle of Hoods and Jerrolds a certain lady who could not appreciate a facetious remark. Her husband once remarked to her with some vexation:

"Why, wife, I don't believe you'd take a

joke if it was pitched at you from a fifteen-inch Dahlgren!"

"Now, John, how foolish," said she, with charming simplicity, "you know they can't fire jokes from a gun."

I do not object to a certain degree of diversity of opinion in regard to facts and conclusions. It is necessary to give spice to the exercises. I would not repress them, except when they are of such a character as to prevent a common interest. I would not have the mathematical, cold and calculating, united with the poetic, warm, emotional. Both would be dissatisfied, and unable to blend. I have known of classes being wrecked on this rock of internal discord. They could not agree in any course of study. There must be harmony in all important chords, though there may be accidentals and musical discords introduced for effect.

I have in my mind now a class that contains eight young men from fifteen to eighteen years of age. Three of them are wild as unbroken colts, and care about as much for religion. They just tolerate the school, but will not listen to any serious conversation. They will not study the lesson or make any prepartion. Two are indifferent but respectful. They could, possibly, be interested by a competent teacher in the pure Bible study. Three are serious, studious, and longing to learn more of the Bible — one almost persuaded to become a Christian, ripe, waiting only to be picked.

This class is paralyzed. A teacher — that is, nine hundred and ninety-nine out of a thousand — cannot interest all by the same course of instruction. For the wild ones, he has to deal in anecdote and pleasing illustration to keep their attention, while the three furthest advanced receive comparatively little benefit — they have grown beyond that stage. If he attempts to satisfy the cravings of the advanced ones, the others are restless and dissatisfied. It is like feeding a new-born babe with roast-beef and plum-pudding. They can't bear it. It is impossible for any ordinary teacher to benefit in any great degree either portion of the class when united. He merely entertains the advanced, or drives away the backward. This is entirely owing to the want of classification, and ten minutes attention of the superintendent in removing one or the other portion of the class, would probably result in the conversion of one and moral improvement of the others. Classification is one of the most important duties of the superintendent.

Where a class starts uninterested and careless, attending merely because they are sent by their parents, I would advise that, for a time at least, they should not be required to commit any lesson; perhaps it would be well merely to request that the lesson be read over during the week. Ask each pupil individually every Sabbath, if he has done this, as the personal question has great influence. I would make the lesson somewhat of a moral lecture, illustrated with anecdotes and incidents — which any good weekly religious paper will supply. Strive, however, in every possible way to induce the pupils to express their own views in their own language. One has a clearer idea of a subject when he has expressed that idea to another. Ask questions, start objections — often so simple that the least cultured can detect their fallacy — and thus inspire discussion. Evade giving your own opinion until you can obtain the sentiment of all in the class. Never tell a pupil what you can induce the pupil to tell you.

Perhaps a real example will best show my meaning on this point. At a very skilfully conducted Bible class, the subject of Christ driving the money changers out of the temple came up. The teacher asked of each his opinion as to what the "scourge of small cords" was, and how Christ obtained it, etc. One thought literally that it was a kind of whip or cat-o'-nine tails, which he had brought on purpose. Another thought that it was merely something that he had taken from the ground to use as a sort of wand, and he did not actually apply it to the backs of the fleeing brokers. Another thought it a rope, which he used veritably and with success. Another amplified, by stating that as the cattle brought for burnt offerings were in the temple, some pieces of rope used in fastening them were lying around, one of which Jesus picked up to give emphasis to his commands. Thus they got inquiring into the matter, each hunting up corroborative passages, discussing the evidences of its being a miracle, etc., and occupied profitably and entertainingly nearly the whole hour over that one passage.

Sometimes it is well to illustrate the lesson with any curiosities you may be able to obtain relating to Bible matters, such as idols, coins, papyrus rolls, relics from ancient cities, etc. Do anything of this nature to make the lesson interesting, for without interest nothing can be accomplished.

As a general rule *perhaps* it is a better plan not to require much to be committed to memory, but to have the time spent in studying into the meaning and teachings of the lesson, its parallel statements, history, effects, etc. I say *perhaps*, for it is a mooted question, upon which I am not at all satisfied. There are many advantages in having the mind stored with Scripture texts, and yet it is more entertaining to study into the character rather, than to commit the words. This point, individual experience must decide.

When practicable, in cases where a class is truly interested and desirous to learn, it is well for each pupil to have a commentary.

For instance, a class of eight have respectively Clarke's, Scott's, and Olshausen's commentaries, Kitto's, Barnes's, Alexander's, and Hodge's notes, and the Annotated Paragraph Bible, by the London Religious Tract Society, (republished by Sheldon & Co., New York.) It will be even better to have two pupils to examine each volume, so that double the number of scholars can be supplied. Study the lesson in the class, each number giving the opinion of his commentator on the obscure passages. This will prove a very entertaining and instructive exercise, and affords ample scope for the teacher's ability, in explaining many little things which no commentary will treat of, and in summing up the testimony of all. This will be a somewhat expensive plan, as commentaries are costly. The "Notes" and the "Annotated Bible" are cheap, however; and those not thus supplied, could have Bibles to turn to the reference passages. On the whole, I think this to be the most sure of success and easy of accomplishment of any plan I know.

There was a class of ladies connected with the late church of Dr. Scott, in New Orleans, on somewhat the same plan, which was conducted by Mr. M., a lawyer of that city. The lesson was usually the history of some Bible personage, and its relations to the truths and doctrines of the Bible. Each pupil would study the lesson at home, with some commentary, and at the class would be questioned as to the facts or teachings. These would, of course, usually be answered according to the opinion of their commentator. Those having different views would suggest their opinions, until the sentiment of the class was obtained. The teacher, with adroit skill, would draw out as much as possible the individual thought and belief. The success of the plan in interesting the class, is shown by the fact that, while it commenced with nine ladies, it increased during the season to ninety-three, and contained all ages, from seventeen to seventy. It was found inconvenient to hold the class on Sunday, and it was transferred to, and continued on Friday afternoons, the session lasting two hours.

Occasionally it may be well to let the class prepare written essays on certain subjects, such as the Sunday question, use of wine, theatre-going, etc., in which they can express their views, and the reasons therefor. But endeavor to discourage all cant and meaningless expressions, so often introduced by young people, because they have heard others do so. Lead them to debate religious matters in a manly, direct, forcible way, as they would political economy, without interspersing it with pious sniffles, to conceal their lack of force. Then, let the class discuss the essay, and decide whether the views of the writer are correct. The teacher should, at the close of the session, state his own opinion, and strive to impress it upon the hearts of the pupils. No matter how much life and vivacity there may be during the exercises — and there should be much — the general tone and influence of the lesson, particularly at the close, should be impressive and subduing.

There is another little plan for interesting the class. Have a place where any member of the class can drop a written question. For instance, each young man writes one, of such a character as, "Do you think the 'latter days' are near at hand?" "Are the present American troubles foretold in prophecy?" "Is it ever right for a non-church member to partake of the sacrament?" or perhaps they may be of a personal character, intended merely for the teacher's eye, speaking of private doubts and trouble. Either the pupils can each select a question — the authorship unknown — to answer in a three-minute essay, or the teacher may reply to such of them as are worthy, before the class or to the writer privately, as may seem best. It is not necessary that the pupils should be competent to write these replies. If they are competent to *try*, it is sufficient. The object is to induce study, and inspire interest, not to prepare articles for the press.*

I think many parents are not sufficiently inclined to urge the attendance of their older children upon the Bible Class. They seldom visit the school, usually speak of it as a very nice children's affair, which saves them some trouble in educating their boys and girls, and in every possible way treat it as beneath the

*Since this plan was suggested in a religious paper, I have learned of its having been adopted in several classes with marked success. Ladies, particularly, who were timid about arguing points, have been ready to defend or assail theories, with their pen, and thus, finally, have been led to express their views *viva voce*.

serious attention of adults. Of course, as the children grow into long dresses and frock coats, they follow their parents' example. It is difficult to secure cheerful obedience when we say, "Go and do," but easy when we beckon, "Come with me."

Parents, it is hard for the superintendent and teachers to do all the work for your children alone, when you, by your example, hold them back. They ask not much from you. They ask merely that you will lend your influence in their attempts to bring *your* family, unbroken, safely to their home in heaven. They ask of you, O father, merely that you will help them restore to you in paradise, the mischievous little curly head you are now stroking. They ask of you, O, mother, merely that you will help them secure to you, your manly, bright-eyed, youngest boy, that you love until tears almost rise at the intensity of your affection. Do they ask too much? It is *your* children they would save.

"A mother's love may prove a snare:
The child she loves so well
Her hand may lead with gentlest care,
Down the steep road to Hell."

CHAPTER XIII.

SUNDAY SCHOOL SEATS.

A VERY important feature in the Sunday School is a suitable form of seat. Much of the restlessness of children is occasioned by the uncomfortable position in which they are placed. Creature comfort is, after all, very desirable, and it is impossible to expect the mind to be at ease, while the body is suffering.

Where the school is held in the church, of course no alteration of the seats can be made. If it meets in the lecture-room, where there are benches or pews, I would have broad, heavy crickets running the whole length of the pew, and forming as it were a false floor. These should be graduated in height to accommodate the size of the pupils in each class. Two of the larger boys will remove them after school, so that they need not interfere with the use of the room by adults. Where the lecture-room has not yet been finished, I would recommend that the seat, which, not knowing any other name, I shall designate the "Booth seat," be introduced. By these seats nearly as many can be seated as by pews, and the room is admirably adapted to the Sunday School. Full directions in regard to this seat are given in a few pages later.

One other, and common form for vestrys, is to have the backs of the seats reversible, like those of the railroad cars, so that in the Sunday School two seats may be caused to face each other. This accommodates the class very well, although half of the school have to sit with their backs to the superintendent, which is, of course, undesirable.

Many buildings, however, are now being erected fcr the exclusive use of the Sunday School, and in these, regard can be paid to the peculiar object to which it is devoted. There seem to be three points to be considered:

1st. An economical seat. 2d. A seat which shall accommodate the pupils with the utmost saving of room, and, 3d. A seat which shall enable all to see the superintendent, and yet allow each class to face, and be within reach of, the teacher.

The most common form, is the semi-circle. These seats are made of various degrees of the arch. They are being gradually lessened in curve, to avoid causing the pupils to twist their backs or necks, in facing the superintendent. The Lee-Avenue school, of Brooklyn, has probably succeeded, as near as is possible, with these seats, in attaining the true proportions.

The engraving on page 223 shows the general form.

The inside circumference of the seat is ten feet. Depth of arch from the chord, two feet eight inches. Height of seat fifteen and a half inches. Breadth of seat ten and a half inches. Height of back fifteen inches, with two back rails. These seats can probably be packed more advantageously in saving room than any others possessing similar advantages. Mr. Johnson, the superintendent of the Lee-Avenue school, has given considerable attention to the subject, and prefers these to any yet introduced. His seats are very expensively made of black walnut. Of course, it is only the form of the seat which it *will be necessary* to imitate.

There is another, comparatively new seat which is growing very popular. It was designed by Mr. Samuel Booth, superintendent of the Hanson Place Methodist Sunday School, Brooklyn, where it is introduced. This is one of the largest and best appointed schools in our country, having a membership of over eight hundred scholars.

THE BOOTH SEAT.

The above cut gives an accurate view of the form of the seats. They have also been introduced into the Plymouth Church Sunday School, and its superintendent, Mr. George A. Bell, speaks in the highest terms of them.

Their dimensions are as follows: Height of seat sixteen and a half inches. (This height is for the *large class seats.*) Height of back fourteen inches, with only one rail to the back. Breadth of seat twelve inches.

The seat is made of a two inch plank, with half an inch hollowed out of the rear of the seat, and gradually rising towards the front, as in the diagram on page 223,which adds greatly to its comfort.

These benches will accommodate seven boys, and occupy a space six feet four inches by four feet two inches; one can calculate that he can seat seven scholars in every thirty-one square feet in his school. This estimate allows also for the aisles.

The features of,—1st. proximity of teachers and pupils; 2d. ability of all to face the superintendent, and 3d. reasonable economy in room, seem to be thoroughly met by this bench. Care must, however, be exercised in placing the seats, not allowing two classes to sit back to back, as thus all the advantages of this seat will be lost. The superintendent's desk should be the point of sight to which all should tend. Usually it is well to have an aisle in the centre of the room, and the seats radiate from it.

In both the Lee-Avenue, and the Booth seats, under one end there is a neat little locker, large enough to hold the Bibles and hymn books, &c., of the class. It is well to have a shelf divide the interior into an upper and lower apartment. In both these seats, the teacher occupies a chair, facing the class, in such a position that he can touch each pupil without moving his position.

Mr. Booth strongly condemns tight board backs to seats for small children, as the spinal column, that position of the body most sensitive to atmospheric changes, becomes heated. It perspires, and when suddenly exposed to the cool air out of doors, is apt to produce serious consequences. The back should be a single rail constructed as lightly as is consistent with strength, and if placed in exactly the right position, will prove as comfortable a support as any. In the arrangement of a room, everything should be as light and open as possible. In painting, a light graining is preferable. Dark colors, and everything like monastic gloom, should be avoided.

He thinks that two and a half feet in width for the centre, and two feet for the side aisles, is enough, where there is an aisle for each tier of benches. This will allow sufficient space for the children to pass out by single file, and certainly it is better to have several narrow, than one broad aisle. Of course, where there is sufficient room, more space is preferable.

For the teachers, some kind of a chair is desirable. In the Lee-Avenue School the chair is fastened to an iron pedestal secured to the floor. The top, an arm chair, turns on a pivot, so that the teacher can face the superintendent, or the class. Where ordinary chairs are used, and the floor of the room is uncarpeted, it is well to glue a thin piece of India rubber on to the bottom of the legs. This will prevent much noise in moving them.

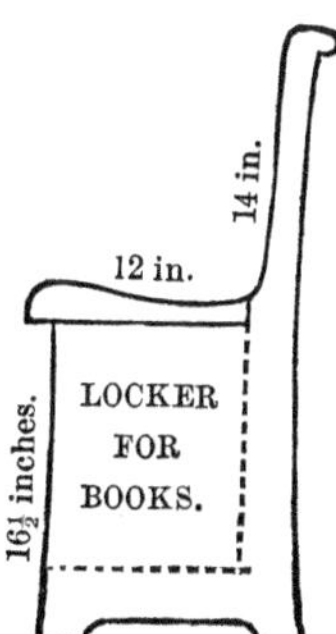

SECTIONAL VIEW OF THE BOOTH SEAT.

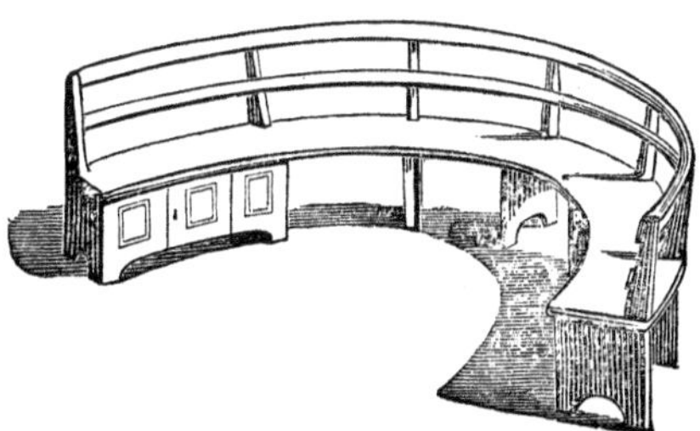

THE SEMI-CIRCLE SEAT.

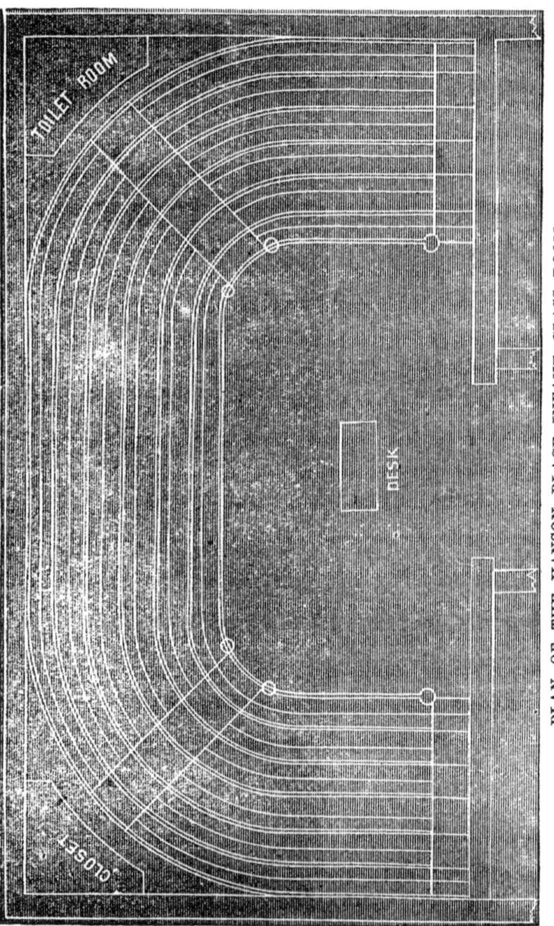

PLAN OF THE HANSON PLACE INFANT CLASS ROOM.

INFANT CLASS SEATS.

The only infant class room I have seen which exactly suited me, is that of the Hanson Place Methodist Sabbath School. In beauty, arrangement, ventilation and yet simplicity, it is apparently perfect. As I am unable to detect an inconvenience or suggest an improvement, I shall merely give a plan and description of it.

It will be seen that it is in the form of a theatre. The first form is raised sixteen inches from the floor, so that the children are not required to tire their necks in looking up at the teacher. From this each tier rises just enough, (say six inches) to allow those in the rear to see over the heads of those in front. The following sectional view will give the dimensions necessary for constructing them. Where the theatre form cannot be used, the same style and size of bench will be applicable to the straight line of seats.

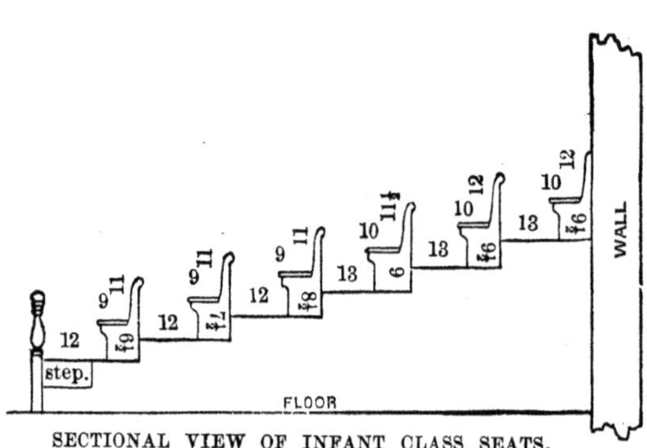

SECTIONAL VIEW OF INFANT CLASS SEATS.

The figures on the plan show the dimensions in *inches.*

If the back of the seat is hollowed out, as described in the Booth seat, it will very much add to their comfort. Where a special room cannot be devoted to the infant class, be sure and have some arrangement of crickets like that descibed in the first part of this chapter. It is impossible to have a sucessful infant class unless the children are made comfortable.

CHAPTER XIV.

STRAY HINTS.

A MAN has a locomotive engine which is finely finished, and securely housed. Now and then he oils it, and paints it, and rubs up the brasses until they shine again. Once or twice a year he takes it from its shed, and lets it run for a few miles. But the pistons have not worn smooth, while the axles are yet rough, and the rust, in spite of all his attention, has formed in unnoticed crevices, and the machine is rheumatic and stiff. It does not run easily.

Supposing the owner comes to you with groans and sighs, asking what more he can do to his engine to make it run? He has watched over it with tender solicitude; never let it out on a damp day, and never after dark; but still it will not run as fast as the old, travel-stained public engines. You would tell him to run his engine in fair weather and foul, and it will work itself into good condition without further trouble on his part.

Now many young Christians are like such engines. They are stiff and rusty. They are much prayed over — which is good, and at which I do not cast a slur; but they are not worked enough to keep their moral joints in order. There are more swords that rust out, than are broken in the strife of battle. There are many young converts who are stunted by lack of healthy exercise. The Sunday school is just the course for them to run on, to acquire this moral strength.

The Sunday school should be used more as a gymnasium for the development of moral muscle among the young. One reason why in great revivals so many backslide, is that they are received into the church with considerable commotion, amidst many prayers, and some excitement. Then, among the multitude, some are forgotten. But little care or attention is given them, and they suffer a relapse. The physician's work is not over when he pronounces his fever patient out of danger. The hours of convalescence are fraught with peril. An unnoticed draught, or too long visit from a friend, or a sudden excitement, may undo all the good. So a young convert must be carefully watched. He must have tender nursing, nutritious food, and gentle exercise, to acquire health. He must *do something*, and in this way "work out his own salvation."

The widow's cruse is still in existence. No one can try to benefit his fellow-men without receiving tenfold more than he gave — though not from man. A faithful teacher in the Sunday School learns more than he imparts.

The Sunday School, therefore, is exactly the place in which to put people to work. Christians should see that its vast benefits in this respect are secured for the improvement of the church. Start the young men either as students in Bible classes or as teachers. If as students, let them occasionally lead in prayer, or have some *active duties*, in visiting the scholars or in gathering in pupils. If they are competent, give them a class. Let them feel the responsibility of their position as teachers. Urge them to attend all the meetings, that they may be surrounded by a religious atmosphere. As in spring-time tender plants are started under cover, surrounded by glass and warmth, until they are strong enough to endure the chance frosts of out-door existence; so the young convert should be encouraged, shielded, and strengthened by all the power of the church until he can withstand the temptations of daily life. This is the object of the church organization.

Thus the church and the school are one, and should be more clearly united in the minds of the congregation. The school is not a parasite, but an important member. The church-members should be kept informed of the condition of the school, and assume the responsibility of it. This is not a useless truism, for it is seldom that the congregation visit the school to see how it is conducted. Parents frequently — even generally — send their children year after year, without putting foot into the school to see what or how they are taught.

A story went the rounds of the papers some years ago, of a man who was raising a pair of colts. He boarded them at a farmer's, some two miles distant, who was charged to take the best of care of them, as they were of a fine breed, and if properly trained would make a valuable span. Every week the owner drove around to see that they were well cared for, and often took friends with him to show them what a magnificent span he would soon have.

This gentleman was the father of two bright boys, whom he sent to school for two years within half a mile of his house. But he had never sufficient time to call at the school, had never conversed with the teacher concerning them, and, indeed, was entirely ignorant of his children's course of instruction.

How many readers have done better in regard to their children at the Sunday School? We all neglect our duties, but have a vague idea that others do better. Pastors should force the Sunday School on the attention of the church. Have parents and friends frequently invited from the pulpit to attend as spectators. Preach upon it, use it in illustrations, and show that it is not an inferior, but merely a different branch of the church.

John Wesley, who established many Sunday Schools in his day, wrote in his diary July 18, 1784, "I find these schools springing up wherever I go. Perhaps God may have a deeper end therein than men are aware of. Who knows but some of these schools may become nurseries for children?"

They have long outstripped Wesley's fondest dreams, and are yet but in their infancy. Those who have given their attention to the subject are fast becoming convinced that God's plans with them are far beyond what has been conceived. They have already begun to be the parents of churches, instead of the offspring. If the salvation of the world is to be attained chiefly by any one agency, the Sunday School is the strongest arm yet raised for its accomplishment.

Hence, what are the duties of the church to the Sunday School? What present difficulties can she alleviate?

In the first place, there should be a more systematic provision for the pecuniary wants of the school. The minister's salary is definitely set, and, theoretically at least, properly raised. The music has a certain sum appropriated for it, and the sexton knows what he is to receive. But the Sunday School is an unprovided-for child, only too frequently cut off with a shilling. Let it be treated as a dutiful child should be, and in the amount to be raised for the year, let its necessities be considered. Appropriate what the school will require, or what the church can give. If it is only one dollar that can be spared, appropriate it, and let the superintendent and teachers be allowed to decide how it shall be expended. Thus they will feel that they are not forgotten. In most churches, after long waiting, the teachers, with great humility, as though asking a personal gift, sue for a collection.

"Touch a man's pocket, and you prick his heart."

Teachers know that the collection yields about half enough to pay existing debts, and they have to supply the deficiency. Teachers are not usually from the wealthier part of the congregation, yet they ordinarily have to support the school. It is a shame that the efficiency of our schools should so often be cramped for want of means. Let the heathen go barefooted a little longer, if necessary, that the Christian heathen may be taught at least morality. You who are piously praying for the Sunday School, and the spread of the Gospel, see to it that your right hand seconds your prayers. We find in "Life-Thoughts" that

"It is not well to pray cream, and live skim milk."

It is well to have a semi-annual Sunday School meeting, at which a report from the school will be presented to the church. It keeps up an interest in the school, inspires anew the teachers, and shows the children that the church really takes a thought for their prosperity.

In large and wealthy churches, I am inclined to think it would be wise to have the entire services of a competent man as superintendent, or rather as children's pastor—paying him, if necessary, a suitable salary. The minister would find him a most useful colleague, and the labors of an energetic man could be well employed in attending to the duties of a city school.

Last Sunday I visited a school in New York, where the superintendent told me that for seven years, at every communion Sabbath but one, there had been members of the school who united with the church. Once there were twenty-four, and frequently there were seven and eight. How many ministers have been as highly blessed? This glorious result is due, under God, to the superintendent. His piety, zeal, and ability in gathering, interesting, and instructing the young, and his skill in selecting teachers and inspiring them to persevere, have made him God's instrument in accomplishing the work. He accepts no teachers who will not pledge themselves to attend the teachers' meetings. He interests the church in the school, and makes them co-workers. Such a course requires force of character, skill, labor, and time. Few can devote so much attention to the object gratuitously, and consequently the fruits are proportionately less. This matter is worthy of serious consideration.

In this connection a few words on the tenure of the superintendent's office may be useful. It is not unfrequent that some very noble man, but inefficient administrator, holds some responsible office in the school. He may not realize his imperfections sufficiently to resign at the proper time; for, as has been observed, "resignation is not a common virtue of office holders." It would break his heart to be ejected, and probably lead to a church quarrel of years duration. No one is willing to incur the odium of opening hostilities, and therefore the matter goes on, the interest of the school suffering accordingly.

The school should be an organized society, with its constitution and by-laws. All the offices should be filled for merely one year. No officer should be elected for the same post for a second term, on less than a two-third vote, and should not be elected for more than five successive terms. After one has been in such an office for five years, he is very apt to have constructed, as it were, a railroad of conduct on which he runs with unvarying sameness. A year's recess will give time and opportunity to look up new plans and improvements, and to see the working of his successor's method. I think this a very important matter, as it is often only in some such way, that a faithful but injudicious officer, can be laid aside or transferred to a more appropriate position, and only by this yearly election, that a really able officer can be assured of his popularity.

All schools should be Mission Schools, where the poor and rich meet together. A celebrated New York school has the poor children meet in a separate room. It is so skilfully managed that the school do not realize it, but the system is bad. This is obvious. It is not necessary for a mistress and her maid to be in the same class, but each should hold an equal position in the school.

Sunday School duties do not cease with the Sabbath any more than do the pastoral obligations. Keep a careful watch over the scholars during the week. I have known of teachers who made their exercises so interesting that they were able to draw together the class on Wednesday evening. Sometimes one can collect a class on a week-day which cannot be gathered on Sunday. Keep a watch for such opportunities. The harder you work, the more interested you will become, and the easier will be the labor.

A visitor should at once be made to feel at home, and urged to attend frequently. This, however, is so universally done, that it does not require enlarging upon. I have found that in a Mission School, a good way to inculcate habits of politeness, is to appoint one of the larger boys as an usher, to escort visitors to their seats, and supply them with singing-books. The usher is considered and treated as one of the officers of the school. It may be well to observe the "rule of rotation in office."

In these days of hurry and bustle, when books of advice have to be written with almost telegraphic terseness, if they are to be read, it is impossible to devote much space to discussing contested points of policy. In this series of essays I have given merely what has seemed to me, to be the best course to pursue. I have received many letters, some opposing my views. As I carefully review these pages for publication, I do not see the necessity of any essential modifications. They are but the guide which controls my own course of conduct week after week in the management of my Mission School, and so far, I have found them sufficient. Still, they are but a single individual's opinion, from which each reader can accept or reject what seems best.

If I can but induce teachers to expend more thought and labor in preparing for their classes; if I can remind them not to neglect their pupils during the week; if I can help them over a few rough places, or bestow a little encouragement where before was despondency, I shall be satisfied.

And you, parents, who are relying so much on the Sunday School for the moral culture of your children, help its prosperity by your own exertions in influence, labor, and money, and thus hasten that glad day when—

"They shall teach no more every man his neighbor, and every man his brother, saying, Know the Lord, for they shall all know me from the least of them to the greatest of them."

INDEX.

www.ingramcontent.com/pod-product-compliance
Lightning Source LLC
LaVergne TN
LVHW010245110826
845151LV00004B/1397

* 9 7 8 1 4 2 5 5 2 2 9 0 2 *